# A Sierra Club Totebook®

# Starr's Guide to the John Muir Trail and the High Sierra Region

by Walter A. Starr, Jr.
**Fold-out map included**

Sierra Club Books • San Francisco

STARR'S GUIDE is published in cooperation with the Sierra Club Foundation by the Sierra Club.

The Foundation was organized to further the scientific, literary, and educational purposes of the club, and welcomes gifts and bequests for this purpose.

The Sierra Club, founded in 1892 by John Muir, has devoted itself to the study and protection of the nation's scenic and ecological resources — mountains, wetlands, woodlands, wild shores, and rivers. All Club publications are part of the nonprofit effort the Club carries on as a public trust. There are some 50 chapters coast to coast, in Canada, Hawaii and Alaska. Participation is invited in the Club's program to enjoy and preserve wilderness everywhere. Address: 730 Polk Street, San Francisco, CA 94109.

*Twelfth revised edition*
Copyright © 1974 by the Sierra Club
Library of Congress Card Catalog No. 67-25840
ISBN: 87156-172-7
Previous editions: Copyright 1934 by Walter A. Starr.
Copyright 1943, 1946, 1951, 1953, 1956, 1959, 1962, 1964, 1967, and 1970 by the Sierra Club.

20   19   18   17   16   15   14   13   12   11
Printed in the United States of America on acid-free paper containing a minimum of 50% recovered waste paper, of which at least 10% of the fiber content is post-consumer waste.

# Foreword to the First Edition

While there may no longer be any undiscovered canyons and lakes in the Sierra Nevada, or any unconquered peaks and passes of importance, and no longer any need to encourage the building of roads and trails, there nevertheless remain countless half-told secrets of the rocks and trees and myriad unexplored aspects of the ever-changing scene. To aid in this further exploration is the purpose of this book.

Walter Starr, Jr., was a life member of the Sierra Club and desired to share in its work. He ardently loved the High Sierra. He could not rest until he had seen it all. And then he wanted others to see it, to enjoy it, and to be inspired by it as he had been. So he made notes of practical directions, then formulated a clear plan for presenting them. Although Pete Starr did not live to take part in the final preparation of his guidebook, so thoroughly was his work done that it was possible to present it very nearly in the form that he had planned. This preparation was done by his father, who has himself an almost unrivaled acquaintance with the High Sierra trails.

In the introduction to this book, Pete Starr wrote:

"By joining the United States Geological Survey maps of the region from Yosemite National Park to the headwaters of the Kern—a distance of more than one hundred and fifty miles—one will observe a continuous strip of blue lakes running down the map immediately west of the Sierra Crest. Through the heart of this blue strip winds the famous John Muir Trail with laterals leading to it from the east and the west, some of them vying with the Muir Trail itself in scenic grandeur."

Acting on the suggestion contained in these lines of his son, Walter Starr had a map made for the book showing the trails and approaches the author so well describes.

As time goes on new trails will be built and old routes will be changed. Further editions will be needed to keep pace with the times; and when they come, be it decades hence, may they still be known as *"Starr's Guide,"* and may the traveler still feel the comradeship of that eager, joyous, and generous youth who loved the beauty of the mountains and wanted others to share his love.

FRANCIS P. FARQUHAR

*San Francisco, 1934*

# Foreword to the Twelfth Edition

More of us are enjoying the High Sierra now than ever before. So many in fact that we are increasingly in danger of loving it to death. We are guests in the high country, not native to the habitat and unable to stay without food and shelter carried up from the lowlands. John Muir could not live long up there on wild onions and Pennyroyal tea, and Indians trading obsidian for salt over the crest did not linger any more than to collect Piñon nuts. Like any guest who expects to return we should respect the local residents, the delicate ecology of plant and animal life in the High Sierra. There are several ways we can preserve the Sierra for those who live there and for our own future enjoyment.

*Tread lightly* as you go; practice minimum impact traveling and camping which will let you enjoy the wilderness without seriously changing or damaging it. Camp with a gas stove to avoid wood fires. Camp at least 100 feet from lakes and streams and keep soaps and detergents out of the water. Dig a small toilet hole well away from camps and water and bury it after use. Don't "improve" campsites; how can you improve on nature? Find your camp instead of building it. Camp on hardened ground, preferably where others have camped before, and especially not in fragile meadows. Leave your campsite cleaner than you found it and pack out all unburnable garbage—burying is no longer acceptable. On the trail don't cut switchbacks, which causes erosion. Give way to pack stock. And please don't litter.

*Spread out.* While popular sections of the Sierra are being trampled, many fine regions of the high country are little noticed. Try an out-of-the-way trail for a more truly wilderness experience. Try the north or south boundary country of Yosemite. Try anywhere on the North Fork of the Kings River, accessible from Courtwright or Wishon Reservoir. Right next to the overused Big Pine Creek and Bishop Pass areas is the little-known high country surrounding Coyote Flat. Also from Wishon Reservoir you can approach the little-known and wildly beautiful Tehipite Valley, in some ways a rival of Yosemite. Or you can get there via Granite Pass out of Cedar Grove in Kings Canyon. South of Cedar Grove the Sugarloaf area deserves more attention. Or try the Hockett-Quinn area approached from Mineral King, Clough Cave, or Atwell Mill. Many other deserted pockets of fine Sierra country await your discovery.

Too many people together are hard on the land. Groups are limited to 25 throughout the Sierra, and fewer in some areas.

*Try a different season.* Fall in the high country is seldom seen but worth the effort. Nights are cold, but the days are often surprisingly warm and the timberline country deserted. Just leave yourself a good exit in case of early season snows. Fish are usually hungry and fall often has the most stable weather of the year.

The adventurous backpacker might also try spring. From late May through June the snowpack is solidified, offering good firm crunchy traveling from sunrise until about noon when it is time to find bare ground to camp on, for the afternoons can be wet and heavy going. A bonus to the spring traveler is a complete absence of mosquitoes. It is a good idea to have an ice axe and know the basics of using it. Cross-country skiers could enjoy late spring touring more than they are now. Winter and early spring, however, are very serious seasons to be abroad in the high country.

*Horses are harder on the land* than people. Try to do without them. Certainly they do far more damage than humans, and they are not indigenous to the alpine habitat. Packers as well as hikers are being held to 1972 use levels, and stock parties are limited to 20 animals. The Mt. Whitney pack station has been at least temporarily closed to help preserve this far over-used trail.

Perhaps a system of human porters will ultimately ease the horse impact. Backpacking has been used to stock dozens of huts in the Alps for years. Human packing in the Sierra would not only reduce the impact but also provide occasional employment for the young backpackers and climbers who frequent the range by summer. Such a system is already in limited use in Big Pine Canyon for stocking high camps of the Palisade School of Mountaineering, where it is quite successful.

The U.S. Forest Service and National Park Service have taken several helpful steps recently toward preserving the Sierra as wilderness. Certainly the most comprehensive of these is the Wilderness Permit system. The Forest Service has taken down all trail signs in some areas, throwing the wilderness traveler back on his own resources of map reading and sense of geography. Along the east side of the Sierra they have lowered some roadheads, leaving a campground at the old roadhead for heavy walk-in use. They are systematically eliminating summer cabins and generally moving the edge of the wilderness further down the canyon. This makes our favorite haunts in the upper basins and along the crest more remote, but it also will help preserve them. Some of the less-used long approaches to the alpine zone now become more attractive by comparison. We should applaud these efforts that are helping to preserve the Sierra.

In preparing this edition of *Starr's Guide* I have taken out some trails abandoned by the National Park Service and Forest Service as well as many cross country "knapsack" routes originally included by Starr himself. Since this may appear as a hindrance to the cross country rambler I would like to explain. In his 1934 Foreword, Francis Farquhar stated that, "To aid in . . . further exploration is the purpose of this book." But further exploration is now no longer necessary, in fact we are in danger of exploring the Sierra to death. Walter Starr saw this danger, and so ends his history of Sierra trails with the thought that, " . . . no more trails should be constructed. To future generations of mountaineers should be left the pleasure, thrill, and experience of pioneering and finding their own routes. . ." As one of those "future generations" we find our numbers and our eagerness threatening the very wilderness which nourishes our sense of wonder. We are surrounded with a proliferation of guidebooks which have even the trailless reaches ever more minutely detailed. This may tempt us onto terrain we are not yet ready for, and certainly destroys in the process our opportunity for "the pleasure, thrill, and experience of pioneering." Yet surely wilderness consists as much of lack of information, the unknown, as it does of lack of roads and people. And surely you will feel your readiness to get off the trail when at length experience brings you to that point. Then you will welcome the chance to explore, which nowadays is so rare. Helping you take your first steps into wilderness is the proper function of this guide and of the trails it describes; the advanced course is best left to the mountains themselves.

Eventually you may want to become a cross country walker to see the Range of Light at its trailless wildest. As I cruise north through the Sierra seeing the wilderness rangers about the districts they patrol I am rarely in need of the trails. . . . Hopefully this book will outlive its usefulness to you as your mountain sense and knowledge of the Sierra develop. By the time you have learned to read the topographic maps well, the trails and trail junctions, the ups and downs and cross country possibilities will stand out to you more clearly there in relief than here as sentences, and be lighter on your back as well.

Wilderness is not just "no bulldozers." It's also not knowing what's over the next rise.

DOUG ROBINSON

*In the shadow of Mt. Starr*
*Rock Creek, Winter 1974*

# Contents

# Walter A. Starr, Sr.
# 1877–1969

With the death of Peter Starr's father it is appropriate to tell briefly of his contributions to the success of *Starr's Guide*. Walter A. Starr, the senior, died August 21, 1969, at the age of 92. His long and happy life, marred temporarily by the early death of Peter, had been exceptionally creative and successful. At 20 he joined the rush for yellow gold on the Klondike in Alaska. With youthful energy he spent three years packing the U.S. Mail down the Yukon in winter. He made more money and accomplished more good than the others who were tearing up that part of Alaska. He returned and years later became Chairman of the Board of a Puget Sound pulp company and a director of one of the largest paper corporations in the world. At the same time, as President of the Sierra Club, he was most effective in stressing the point that while some trees were crops, those in National Parks and dedicated Wilderness Areas should never be logged under any pretext.

But it was *Starr's Guide* that held his principal interest the last 36 years. He edited, published and copyrighted the first edition, as his contribution to the knowledge and protection of the High Sierra. That edition lasted almost ten years. Then, through nine more editions over a period of 24 years, Walter substantially financed the printing costs so that the Guide could be distributed at minimum cost to all who love and want to protect the Sierra. Now Walter has generously left an endowment with the Sierra Club Foundation, for the continued publication of the Guide.

The vitality and value of *Starr's Guide* after 37 years, is an appropriate tribute to Peter and his father, whose foresight has made these continuing editions possible.

RICHARD M. LEONARD

*San Francisco, 1970*

# Key to Trail Descriptions and Map References

*Elevations and Distances are indicated thus: Mirror Lake* (4,100—2.4); the first figure gives the elevation in feet above sea level; the second the distance in miles and tenths of miles from place above, or place where last stated. When distance only is given it is shown thus: (10.1). When elevation only is given it is shown thus: (8,500).

When reference is given such as peak 12,820 or lake 10,132, the figures are the elevations shown on the U.S. Geological Survey maps which identify many unnamed peaks and lakes.

*Trail Designations are indicated thus:* (18), and refer to corresponding numbers appearing on the special map prepared for use with this Guide.

## Abbreviations

*Other Map References, followed by identifying numerals, are:*

| | |
|---|---|
| AR | Alternate Route |
| EA | Eastern Approach |
| EL | Eastern Lateral |
| HST | High Sierra Trail |

*Warning:* Early in the summer and in years of heavy snowfall, high passes and steep slopes may be dangerous except for experienced mountaineers properly equipped for climbing on snow.

# Introduction

## Advice to Travelers—Maps and Information

The grand crescendo of the Sierra Nevada begins in the Yosemite National Park and culminates in the southern group of fourteen-thousand-foot peaks at the headwaters of the Kings River and the Kern.

On the eastern side the mountain range drops off rapidly losing from 6,000 to 10,900 feet, into Mono Basin and Owens Valley. This is because the eastern side is the fault scarp made by the displacement of the earth's crust in the upheaval of the range. Owing to erosion, this face is greatly sculptured with deep canyons and sharp intervening ridges, sometimes highly colored, presenting a grand appearance from U.S. Highway 395, which runs along its base. On the western (or San Joaquin Valley) slope, the mountain range rises gradually from foothills to the crest, making high mountain travel up and down the range and in proximity to the crest more practicable on that side.

By joining the United States Geological Survey maps of the region from Yosemite National Park to the headwaters of the Kern—a distance of more than one hundred and fifty miles—one will observe a continuous strip of blue lakes running down the map immediately west of the Sierra Crest. Through the heart of this blue strip winds the famous John Muir Trail with laterals leading to it from the east and the west, some of them vying with the Muir Trail itself in scenic grandeur. Except for the short portion of the route lying between Donohue Pass and Island Pass, the Muir Trail traverses the headwaters of the western slope of the watershed of the Sierra.

The chief mode of travel through the High Sierra is on foot or horseback, with knapsack or pack train. It is to be hoped that this marvelous region traversed by the Muir Trail will never be opened up by motor roads, but will be kept inviolate, reserved as a wilderness area. This does not mean that travel amid the wonders of this region should not be popularized and made possible by good and well-kept trails. I do not hold with some lovers of the high mountains, who have in mind the crowded conditions in such places as Yosemite Valley, that this should not be done. For the more general the public interest in the high mountains, the easier it should be to obtain appropriations for trail building and repair and to prevent destruction of the resources and beauty of the mountains. Only those who appreciate the high mountains will take the trouble to visit them so long as there are no automobile roads. I am therefore in sympathy with those who believe in making the High Sierra region accessible and its beauty known, but who insist that automobile roads be kept out of it, believing that to be the only way to preserve it.

John Muir frequently condemned writers, overenthusiastic about their favorite regions, who drew exaggerated comparisons prejudicial to other places of undoubted beauty. Nevertheless, the high mountain region traversed by the trail named for him is unquestionably the finest mountain area in the state. I am an ardent lover of the mountains and admire all mountain scenery; but while the type of country in the lower and middle Sierra pleases me, the High Sierra fascinates and thrills me. The forests are finer and more extensive in the lower Sierra, but thick forests tend to blot out the surrounding mountains. The beauty of trees is less apparent when they are massed closely together than when they are growing sparsely in isolated groups, with more individuality, contrasted strikingly against the surrounding landscape.

Towering cliffs like those of Pate Valley, Simpson Meadow, the canyons of Kings River, Paradise Valley, and the Kern, have charm. But although typical of the finest in the middle Sierra, to me they soon become monotonous. They fail to sustain a fascinated interest as do the peaks and cliffs in the regions near the crest, with their individuality and variety.

In the vacation months, when it is hot, dry, and dusty in the middle and lower Sierra, it is springtime in my strip of blue lakes through which the Muir Trail winds. The snow has just left the ground. The meadows are a luscious green and dazzle one with their flowers. The lights and shadows are intense. The air is fresh and invigorating. There is variety, contrast, color. In short, the rugged grandeur, freshness, and variety of the High Sierra please me most. When viewed from the summit of a typical Sierra peak, the high mountain region appears to be a forbidding desolate expanse of granite basins and cliffs. The small valleys, meadows, and forests which lie hidden between them, contrasting so delightfully with their rugged surroundings, do not meet the eye. The High Sierra, with its meadows, streams, and lakes, is friendly and hospitable in summer. A few spirits are oppressed by the mightiness of the high mountains. They prefer the more friendly, peaceful type of scenery in the lower mountains. But this is a matter of individual taste rather than a subject for argument.

Most of the literature concerning the High Sierra region consists of general descriptions of its beauties and personal impressions and experiences of the writers. This makes delightful reading, but is of little practical use in planning trips into the the mountains. The United States Geological Survey Maps and the *Sierra Club Bulletin* are of great assistance. Doubtless the chief factor in stimulating interest in the High Sierra has been the Sierra Club, inspired by the leadership and spirit of its first president, John Muir.

I have become convinced, by my personal experience in these mountains while on many trips during recent years, of the utility that a guidebook of this nature will have for those who would see them.

### Advice to Travelers

Only those capable of mountain travel at high altitudes should undertake trips into the High Sierra regions without a guide or some companion familiar with the conditions to be met. The most favorable time of the year is between July 15th and September 15th, depending on snow depths, which vary considerably from year to year. Fall travel can be very pleasant as late as the middle of November. As long as one is prepared for the crisp nights and keeps in mind a course of retreat in case of snowstorm, he can enjoy this seldom-seen season in the high country. Cross-country skiers might consider trying spring as well, but winter in the Sierra is a serious proposition.

While it is possible to travel from one end of the Muir Trail to the other in a single trip, I consider it a far better plan to explore the region traversed by the trail in sections, taking a different one each trip. There are so many side trips to take and such wonderful country to see along the route that many seasons should be planned for them. Each year one can look forward to enjoying a new part of the High Sierra. When animals are used this method also helps solve the problem of returning them. Many of the laterals or approaches to the Muir Trail are as fine as the trail itself, and by properly planning the trips one may use different routes to reach the high regions from year to year, perhaps going in over one lateral and coming out on another. Many circuits of this kind can be arranged.

Another plan is to pack in to a permanent camp, favorably situated, from which to make excursions into the surrounding regions. A more complete camp outfit may then be taken, including a tent.

Parties doing their own packing should know how to "throw a hitch" properly. Packs should be evenly balanced to avoid sore backs and firmly secured to prevent shifting. Throw a canvas over the pack before roping to keep out dust and to shed rain. Do not overload—150 to 175 lbs. for horse or mule, and 75 to 100 lbs. for a burro, are enough on mountain trails, and less should be carried over rough going. Horses and mules must be kept shod, and shoes, nails, and shoeing outfit should be included in the pack. Both are likely to stray while feeding, horses more than mules, and hobbles will help to prevent this. Hang a bell on your stock when you camp to help keep track of them. Burros, while slow, offer many advantages, especially in rough going and on side trips off trails. They will take their proper load over rocks and ledges where horses and mules cannot follow. They can subsist upon meager pasturage where the larger animals would starve. They do not wear shoes, and can be bought much more cheaply. The care and packing of animals require experience and knowledge of the character of the animals used.

About two miles an hour is the average speed made by pack animals on mountain trails—more on level stretches, and less on climbs and steep descents. Burros are slower. A fast hiker can average three miles an hour, but a two-mile average will be found by most to be enough.

The outfit is a question on which there is a wide range of opinion, but I believe a few things should be mentioned as indispensable. Whether hiking or using pack stock, travel as light as you can. You can get along with less than you think. (*Ed.:* See *Walking Softly in the Wilderness: The Sierra Club Guide to Backpacking,* John Hart. Sierra Club, 1977).

Plastic water buckets are convenient and easy to pack. A folding reflecting oven is very handy. Place it beside the fire and your bread or biscuits can be baking while the balance of the meal is cooking over the fire. On short trips bread may be taken along, but it is bulky and soon gets stale. Some fire irons to place across a couple of rocks are a great convenience. Cooking utensils should "nest" into the least space.

Waterproof tarps should be taken with a pack outfit to protect supplies from rainstorms and to provide a lean-to for shelter in camp. Nothing is more miserable than a wet camp, and that can easily be avoided. Large tents are too cumbersome for extended trips, but small one- to two-man tents are useful for emergency shelter. Each member of a pack party should have a good light knapsack, not only for knapsack trips, but for carrying a sweater or poncho, lunch, and other articles while on the trail or climbing.

Go light on your supply of clothes and personal effects. After all, it is hard to beat jeans. You will need a warm parka or sweater for cool evenings and camp use. In fact, one or the other should always be with you. Take a light rainponcho, for thunder showers must be expected, and wet clothes can make you cold and miserable. Footgear is perhaps the most important item. Many a trip is spoiled by sore feet. Wear two pair of socks, a light pair next to the skin with woolen socks over them. This will avoid blisters and chafing. They should fit perfectly without wrinkles. Shoes should be large enough to be comfortable with the double socks, but not too large, and the leather should be oiled and flexible. For trails, climbing and snow, use leather hiking boots or shoes with vibram rubber-cleated soles. Smooth rubber shoes are a positive danger on snow or ice or any wet surface. If you set out to traverse glaciers or to make steep snow climbs, a good ice axe will prove of great assistance and add to your safety—once you have learned to use it. (*Ed.:* See *Wilderness Skiing,* Lito Tejada-Flores and Allen Steck. Sierra Club, 1972).

A good sleeping bag with a rainproof square of waterproof cloth (7×7) (new lightweight materials such as nylon are now available), to serve as ground cover and bag cover when folded over, makes the best bed. Cold nights must be provided for in high altitudes.

Bags of mummy-case design, filled with down, are excellent.

A few essentials of personal equipment which should be in the outfit are: dark glasses to protect the eyes in snow and glare; a flashlight and extra bulbs and batteries; ointment for sunburn or cracked lips; surgical bandages, disinfectant, moleskin, and adhesive tape; a good pocket knife and a box to carry matches and keep them dry. A few yards of fine-mesh mosquito netting, Cutter insect repellent, and some gloves may add much to your comfort at times. Have with you a good map, including the topographic map of the U.S.G.S. covering the region to be traversed. If you are inexperienced in providing yourself with a proper outfit for your trip, consult someone who has had previous experience in the High Sierra and take his advice.

While the question of provisions is mainly one of individual taste, some suggestions are in order. The more your food supply is concentrated (that is, without water content) the smaller and lighter the pack will be. But care should be used to see that some foods are taken which are bulky when cooked and satisfy large appetites, avoiding those requiring long boiling. Remember that water boils at a lower temperature in high altitudes, so that beans and such are slow and difficult to cook. Such food as crackers, cheese, dried or jerked beef, sweet chocolate, nuts, raisins, dried fruits, packaged trail drinks, and other concentrated foods should be provided for trail or climbing lunches. (Mountaineering shops now stock a wide variety of specialty foods, but ingenuity and the supermarket can be as light and much cheaper.) As for quantities and proportions, again consult someone of experience. (*Ed.:* See *Simple Foods for the Pack,* Vikki Kinmont and Claudia Axcell. Sierra Club, 1976. See also *Cooking for Camp and Trail,* Hasse Bunnelle with Shirley Sarvis. Sierra Club, 1972; and *Food for Knapsackers,* Hasse Bunnelle with Winnie Thomas. Sierra Club, 1971.)

While bears are usually harmless to humans, it is wise to cache provisions carefully when leaving camp, if they are known to be about. Rodents, marten, and porcupine may also raid supplies. Suspended out of reach on a rope between two trees, food may be safely left.

Remember to obey the national park and national forest rules and regulations, which are few but important. Secure wilderness permits and obtain necessary maps and information from district rangers in the parks and forests. (Camp only at designated sites in Yosemite National Park.) No wood fires are permitted now at many campsites, and gas stoves will be needed there for cooking. Their use is strongly encouraged everywhere in the Sierra to conserve wood, an important part of the minimum impact idea.

Burn food scraps, paper, and other combustible refuse. Bury all human waste. *Keep and leave your camp cleaner than when you found it.* Do not pollute the water. Carry foil and other non-burnable trash out of the mountains with you; do not bury it. Leave all natural features undisturbed; remove all wires and nails from trees. Do not cut blazes on trees and do not erect any new ducked trails. Do not drop papers along the trail. No firearms in national parks; and no cats or dogs. California State fishing licenses are required.

While no attempt will be made here to describe routes of ascent of the many peaks which may be climbed from points along the Muir Trail, some of the most accessible peaks will be mentioned which give the finest views and whose summits can be reached safely without climbing equipment or much previous experience. It frequently happens that the best views are obtained from the easiest peaks. (See *The Climber's Guide to the High Sierra,* Steve Roper. Sierra Club, 1976.)

## *Maps and Information Available*

Consult the special map prepared for use with this book.

The National Park Service and the National Forest Service issue maps and information for the use of the general public. These do not show topography, but since they are often updated they have the latest and most accurate trail locations. The Department of the Interior issues U.S.G.S. topographic maps which are of great value because they show the shape of the terrain.

The following list covers maps, information, and literature useful to the traveler in the regions covered by this book:

(A) Publications by the Department of the Interior, which may be obtained free on application to the National Park Service, Washington, D.C., or from the Regional Office, 450 Golden Gate Avenue, San Francisco, or at the office of any park superintendent—

guide maps and circulars of general information which list other publications of interest.

(B) Maps issued by the Department of Agriculture, with information on reverse side, through the Forest Service, which can be obtained free from the Regional Office of the U.S. Forest Service, 630 Sansome Street, San Francisco, and from ranger stations: Toiyabe, Inyo, Sierra, Sequoia and Stanislaus national forests.

(C) Topographic (U.S.G.S.) maps, issued by the Department of the Interior, and sold by the Director of the United States Geological Survey, Washington, D.C. They can also be obtained at the Geological Survey office at 555 Battery Street, San Francisco, at many stationery and engineers' supplies stores and in the parks, at a nominal price.

The U.S.G.S. publishes a 15 Minute Series of quadrangles (scale 1:62500 or about 1 inch to the mile, contour interval 80 feet on most, 40 feet on some). Land forms and lakes are depicted with extreme accuracy. The 15 Minute Series of quadrangles which cover high mountain regions are: Tower Peak, Matterhorn Peak; Hetch Hetchy Reservoir, Tuolumne Meadows, Mono Craters; Yosemite, Merced Peak, Devils Postpile, Mt. Morrison; Kaiser Peak, Mt. Abbott, Mt. Tom; Blackcap Mountain, Mt. Goddard, Big Pine; Tehipite Dome, Marion Peak, Mt. Pinchot; Giant Forest, Triple Divide Peak, Mt. Whitney; and Kaweah, Mineral King, and Kern Peak.

Two large U.S.G.S. maps (scale 1:125000) are available covering both National Parks. The Yosemite National Park includes the Dardanelles, Bridgeport, Yosemite and Mt. Lyell quadrangles. The Sequoia-

Kings Canyon National Parks includes portions of Tehipite, Mt. Whitney, Kaweah and Olancha quadrangles. The elevations on these maps are not as accurate or up-to-date as on the 15 Minute Series of quadrangles, and the contour intervals are larger, but these two maps taken together cover most of the High Sierra region covered by this guide and make, especially in the shaded relief versions, a fine wall hanging for winter evening musings.

This edition of the Guide uses the elevations from the 15 Minute Series of quadrangles. When unnamed peaks are referred to for spotting locations on the map, two elevations are given, the old ones (from 1:125000 topographic maps) in brackets.

(D) Air photos of much of Toiyabe, Inyo, Sierra, and Sequoia national forests and of Yosemite National Park are sold by the Regional Office of the Forest Service in San Francisco. These photos overlap each other enough to provide three-dimensional, large-scale coverage of a large part of the High Sierra traversed by the John Muir Trail. With brief training one may read the three dimensions without stereoscopic equipment. The trail itself is rarely discernible, but one may still count the trees, as well as reconnoiter cross-country routes and select off-trail campsites and grazing. The photos are of so large a scale that many are required to cover extended trips, and are thus probably out of question for energetic knapsackers.

# Your Wilderness Permit

The Sierra has become a very popular wilderness lately; 10,000 people, for example, visited the summit of Mt. Whitney in the summer of 1972. The National Parks and Forests of the Sierra have decided that limiting the number of people in the back country is the best way to preserve both the delicate alpine ecology and the personal values of the wilderness experience. So they have worked out a cooperative system of Wilderness Permits to let as many people as possible visit the Sierra without damaging it in the process beyond its ability to recover. Not as many of us will go up Mt. Whitney this year, but those who go will be able to feel a bit more quiet space around them, and the Whitney landscape will benefit as well.

Wilderness permits are issued free of charge at the ranger station nearest your point of entry into the wilderness. You are required to have one for each trip you make into the wilderness. Every entrance point has a daily limit. Onion Valley/Kearsarge Pass, for example, allows 120 people per day. Up to half of the daily quota of permits can be issued by mail, but only before July 1. The rest are given out on a first-come-first-serve basis not more than 24 hours before the trip starts. Yosemite, however, has no reservation system. A permit is good for one trip, even if it ends far from the issuing station in another park or forest. Once in the wilderness you may travel as you please.

Where to get wilderness permits west of the Sierra:

## Yosemite

Valley Visitor Center
Happy Isles Visitor Center
Wawona Ranger Station
Tuolumne Meadows Ranger Station
Mather or Hetch Hetchy Ranger Station
Big Oak Flat or Crane Flat Ranger Station

## Sierra National Forest

Minarets Ranger Station, North Fork
Oakhurst Ranger Station
Clover Meadows Ranger Station
Minaret Work Center, north of Mammoth Pool
Eastwood Visitor Information Center, Huntington Lake
High Sierra Ranger Station, Edison-Florence Lake Road
Pineridge Ranger Station, Big Creek
Dinkey Creek Ranger Station at Shaver Lake
Kings River Ranger Station, Sanger

## Sequoia-Kings Canyon

At each trailhead in Kings Canyon (Cedar Grove)
Giant Forest
Ash Mountain Entrance Station

Where to get wilderness permits east of the Sierra:

Mono Lake Ranger Station, on Tioga Road
Mammoth Ranger Station
Twin Lakes Entrance Station, Lake Mary
Minaret Entrance Station, Devils Postpile road

Rock Creek Entrance Station, upper Rock Creek
Bishop Creek Entrance Station, west of Bishop
White Mountain Ranger Station, Bishop
Onion Valley Entrance Station, west of Independence
Mt. Whitney Ranger Station, Lone Pine

# PART I:
# Yosemite
# National Park Region

This region includes Yosemite Valley (often referred to simply as Yosemite) and Tuolumne Meadows and their back-country—the headwaters of the Merced River and the Tuolumne River. These are, in the words of John Muir, "two of the most songful streams in the world."

## Sec. 1.   General Information—Yosemite National Park

*Reached by bus:* From Merced and Fresno.

*Reached by auto:* Highway 140 (the all-weather highway) from Merced; Wawona road from Fresno and Madera (Highway 41); Big Oak Flat Road (Highway 120), leaving U.S. Highway 99 at Manteca; Tioga Road from U.S. Highway 395 on the east side of the Sierra via Tioga Pass and Tuolumne Meadows—closed during winter snows.

*Accommodations:* Yosemite Valley all year; Wawona, Tuolumne Meadows, and High Sierra Camps in summer.

*Camping:* Permitted only in areas designated by the Park Service. All references to "camping" *in this section* of Starr's Guide indicate designated areas.

*Outfitting points:* Supplies, saddle and pack stock, guides: Yosemite, Wawona, Mather Station, Tuolumne Meadows—inside the park—and authorized packers in national forests adjoining Yosemite. (See Sec. 9 and Part II, Secs. 3, 6, 12). No grazing of stock is allowed in Yosemite Valley, but you can arrange with the Yosemite Park and Curry Company for corral and feed at the stables, located at the upper end of the Valley on Merced River, one mile downstream from Happy Isles.

Yosemite Valley is the premier scenic attraction of the state. Many fine descriptions and detailed maps are available of this region, which, therefore, need not be covered in this guidebook. Yosemite was ever close to the heart of John Muir, and it is fitting that it should be the point from which the John Muir Trail starts.

The route adopted for the Muir Trail from Yosemite Valley to Tuolumne Meadows is the Sunrise Trail via Nevada Fall and Cathedral Pass. Alternate routes are Tenaya Lake Trail (AR 1), Merced Lake-Tuoloumne Pass Trail (AR 3), Merced Lake-Vogelsang Pass Trail (AR 4).

## Sec. 2. The John Muir Trail

### *Yosemite Valley to Tuolumne Meadows*

| *via Sunrise Trail* | El. above Sea level | Dist. from pt. above | Dist. from Yosemite | Dist. to Tuol. Mdws. |
|---|---|---|---|---|
| Happy Isles . . . . . . . . . . . . . . . . . . . . . . . | 4,035 | 0.0 | 0.0 | 23.9 |
| Mist Trail . . . . . . . . . . . . . . . . . . . . . . . . . | 4,550 | 1.0 | 1.0 | 22.9 |
| Panorama Trail (Nevada Fall) . . . . . . | 5,950 | 2.3 | 3.3 | 20.6 |
| Little Yosemite (trail junction) . . . . . . | 6,150 | 1.4 | 4.7 | 19.2 |
| Half Dome Trail . . . . . . . . . . . . . . . . . | 7,000 | 1.5 | 6.2 | 17.7 |
| Clouds Rest Trail . . . . . . . . . . . . . . . . . | 7,200 | 0.5 | 6.7 | 17.2 |
| Merced Lake High Trail . . . . . . . . . . . | 8,100 | 1.9 | 8.6 | 15.3 |
| Forsyth Trail . . . . . . . . . . . . . . . . . . . . | 8,150 | 0.1 | 8.7 | 15.2 |
| Long Meadow (Sunrise Camp) . . . . . | 9,400 | 5.0 | 13.7 | 10.2 |
| Echo Creek Trail . . . . . . . . . . . . . . . . . | 9,450 | 1.0 | 14.7 | 9.2 |
| Cathedral Pass . . . . . . . . . . . . . . . . . . . | 9,700 | 1.0 | 15.7 | 8.2 |
| Cathedral Lake Trail . . . . . . . . . . . . . . | 9,500 | 2.1 | 17.8 | 6.1 |
| Tuolumne Meadows (trail junction) . | 8,550 | 3.0 | 20.8 | 3.1 |
| Glen Aulin Trail (Soda Springs) . . . . . | 8,600 | 1.5 | 22.3 | 1.6 |
| Tuolumne Meadows Ranger Station . | 8,700 | 1.6 | 23.9 | 0.0 |

The John Muir Trail starts from the upper end of Yosemite Valley where the Merced River comes rushing down the canyon to enter the valley through the beautiful

*Happy Isles* (4,035—0.0), where the Nevada Fall Trail starts. This trail proceeds up the left bank (a horse trail leads up along the right side) of the Merced River, later crossing by a bridge (fine view of Vernal Fall) to the right bank. Upon reaching the junction of the

*Mist Trail* (4,550—1.0) (which leaves our route on the left, following up the river and ascending a cliff to the top of Vernal Fall, which is impassable to animals) we ascend the south wall of the canyon, enjoying beautiful views of the waterfall as we approach the rim of

*Nevada Fall* (5,950—2.3). Here we meet the Panorama Trail via Illilouette Fall from Glacier Point (5).

We cross the Merced River just above Nevada Fall and have a thrilling view from the brink into the mist-filled chasm below. We then follow the Merced Lake Trail (26) to the lower end of

*Little Yosemite Valley* (6,150—1.4) (camping and grazing) where we leave the Merced Lake Trail and proceed north on the Sunrise Trail which follows the route of the old Indian trail from Wawona to Mono Lake. After passing the south face of Half Dome we come to the junction of

*Half Dome Trail* (7,000—1.5) which leaves our route to the west, proceeds to the saddle at the rim of Tenaya Canyon, between Half Dome and Clouds Rest, and ascends via a cable stairway to the flat summit of the dome.

We continue on the Sunrise Trail to the junction of the

*Clouds Rest Trail* (7,200—0.5), which ascends 3.8 miles northward to the top of Clouds Rest with its superb view. We proceed eastward to Sunrise Creek, and after crossing it, follow up its forested slopes. A short distance south is Moraine Dome (fine views). Continuing up Sunrise Creek we come to the junction of the

*Merced Lake (High) Trail* (8,100—1.9) which leaves our route to the east (26b) and descends via Echo Creek (camping and grazing in Echo Valley) to Merced Lake—distance 5.6 miles. Nearby is the junction of the

*Forsyth Trail* (8,150—0.1). The Forsyth Trail (19) branches north to Tenaya Lake (7.1) to meet AR 1. We follow up Sunrise Creek to its headwaters and then go along the eastern side of the long ridge of Sunrise Mountain, through a beautiful country, at the headwaters of the west branch of Cathedral Fork of Echo Creek in

*Long Meadow* (9,400—5.0) (no grazing). Here is the Sunrise High Sierra Camp, where a trail goes west, climbs over Sunrise Mountain, and descends past the three Sunrise Lakes to meet the Forsyth Trail (19) (9,500—2.5), which descends steeply to Lake Tenaya (8,150—2.5). The Muir Trail continues up Long Meadow to a junction with the

*Echo Creek Trail* (9,450—1.0), which descends to the Cathedral Fork of Echo Creek and then follows down its canyon to a junction with the Merced Lake Trail (6,700—7.0) (see Sec. 4). Leaving Long Meadow we ascend past Columbia Finger, then between Tresidder Peak (10.700), nearby and easily climbed for a fine view, and Echo Peaks to

*Cathedral Pass* (9,700—1.0). From here we can look back over the sweeping panorama of the upper basin of the Merced River and its many surrounding peaks. Nearby, to the east, rise the spectacular knife-blade summits of Matthes Crest. Just north of the pass we come to a glacial basin, at the headwaters of Tenaya Creek, which is dominated by the towering spire of Cathedral Peak (10,940). Here lies one of the Cathedral Lakes in a setting made beautiful by its surrounding three peaks. Leaving the basin we pass the junction of the

*Cathedral Lake Trail* (9,500—2.1), by which it is 0.5 mile west to the lower Cathedral Lake (camping and grazing), and then start down the long descent on the forested slopes below Cathedral Peak toward Tuolumne Meadows. Just before arriving at the level meadow where our trail dead-ends at the Tioga Road, we meet the

*Tenaya Lake-Tuolumne Meadows Trail* (8,500—3.0) (see Sec. 3), which now becomes our route. Crossing Budd Creek on a bridge we travel eastward about a mile to where the trail forks. Taking the north-branching Soda Springs Trail we meet and cross the Tioga Road where the old road, coming across the meadow from the river, meets it. Now only a trail, we follow it across the meadow and cross the Tuolumne River on the old bridge to the north bank. Nearby is Parsons Memorial Lodge recently donated to the Park by the Sierra Club along with a campground which is now devoted to walk-in backpacker use, and the famous Soda Springs. Here is the junction with the

*Glen Aulin Trail* (8,600—1.5) (see Sec. 3), which goes down the river to Glen Aulin (4.8). We follow the old road eastward, again cross the new Tioga Road, and proceed to

*Tuolumne Meadows Ranger Station* (8,700—1.6). Nearby is the Tuolumne Meadows Lodge. (Extensive campground 1 mile south.)

## Sec. 3. Alternate Route No. 1

### *Tenaya Lake—Tuolumne Meadows Trail*

| Yosemite V. to Tuolumne Meadows | El. above Sea level | Dist. from pt. above | Dist. from Yosemite | Dist. to Tuol. Mdws. |
|---|---|---|---|---|
| Mirror Lake ..................... | 4,100 | 0.0 | 0.0 | 21.4 |
| Tenaya Lake Trail ................ | 4,500 | 1.0 | 1.0 | 20.4 |
| North Dome Trail ................ | 6,900 | 2.7 | 3.7 | 17.7 |
| May Lake Trail ................... | 7,600 | 1.6 | 5.3 | 16.1 |
| Ten Mile Meadow ................ | 8,000 | 2.5 | 7.8 | 13.6 |
| Tenaya Lake ..................... | 8,150 | 3.6 | 11.4 | 10.0 |
| Tuolumne Meadows (trail junction) . | 8,550 | 8.0 | 19.4 | 2.0 |
| Lyell Fork Trail (Muir Trail) ....... | 8,600 | 2.0 | 21.4 | 0.0 |

We start forth from

*Mirror Lake* (4,100—0.0) at the lower end of Tenaya Canyon, which is dominated by the sheer western face of Half Dome. Above the lake our route proceeds a short way through woods up Tenaya Canyon and then zigzags 2,500 feet up the steep north wall to the rim of the canyon between Basket Dome and Mount Watkins. Interesting views of Half Dome and Tenaya Canyon are enjoyed during the ascent. (This may be a dry trail in late summer.) At the rim of Tenaya Canyon, Snow Creek is soon reached, where we pass the junction of the

*North Dome Trail* (6,900—3.7). The North Dome Trail continues up the west bank of Snow Creek, while our route fords the stream and follows up the east bank (camping). Later an ascent is made up one of the branches of Snow Creek to the junction of the

*May Lake Trail* (7,600—1.6) which branches north from our route to May Lake High Sierra Camp (9,300—5.2) (camping). From May Lake this trail (18b) leads circuitously to Ten Lakes (9,200—14.0) (see Sec. 7), and to Glen Aulin High Sierra Camp (7,800—7.5) (see p. 42). Mt. Hoffmann rises from the west shore of the lake. Our trail continues upward to the top of a dividing ridge and descends the east side to

*Ten Mile Meadow* (8,000—2.5). Here good grazing and fine flowers in season are to be found. Above the meadow we pass Hidden Lake (not visible from the trail). We now ascend over a long open ridge (fine view of upper Tenaya Canyon) and, after descending, pass an unnamed lake and traverse a fine wooded meadow (good grazing). Here we come to a trail junction with four other trails, described below, at the western end of

*Tenaya Lake* (3,150—3.6) (50-site walk-in campground at west end of lake). This "lake of the shining rocks" is one of the most beautiful glaciated lakes in the High Sierra. The shallow west end of the lake is known for its unusually warm Sierra swimming. The Tioga Road skirts the north shore of the lake. From the trail hub at its western end start four trails. The Forsyth Trail (19), which leads to the Muir Trail, via Sunrise Lakes, in Long Meadow (5.0), or on Sunrise Creek (7.0) (see Sec. 2); the McGee Lake Trail to Glen Aulin (7.6) (see p. 42); the May Lake Trail, using the old Tioga Road (4.0); and the new trail to Tuolumne Meadows, which follows along the southern side of Tenaya Lake, thence up Cathedral Creek to its forks, whence it follows the Tioga Road on the south side to

*Tuolumne Meadows Trail Junction* (8,550—8.0), where we meet the Muir Trail approaching the Tioga Road and our trail becomes its route for about a mile (see Sec. 2). After crossing Budd Creek we travel along a forested slope back from the meadow, pass the junction of the north-branching Soda Springs Trail, cross the Elizabeth Lake Trail leading to the Tuolumne Meadows Campground and store, to arrive at a junction with the

*Lyell Fork Trail* (Muir Trail) (8,600—2.0), which goes up the Lyell Fork of the Tuolumne River. Three quarters of a mile beyond the junction a trail branches north to cross the Lyell and Dana forks of the river. From it trails branch leading to the Tuolumne High Sierra Camp (1.7) and the Ranger Station (1.9).

### McGee Lake–Glen Aulin Trail (20-21)

| Tenaya Lake to Tuolumne Meadows | El. above Sea level | Dist. from pt. above | Total distance | |
|---|---|---|---|---|
| Tenaya Lake . . . . . . . . . . . . . . . . . . . . . . | 8,150 | 0.0 | 0.0 | 11.9 |
| Junction May Lake Trail . . . . . . . . . . | 8,700 | 3.0 | 3.0 | 8.9 |
| McGee Lake . . . . . . . . . . . . . . . . . . . . | 8,100 | 3.3 | 6.3 | 5.6 |
| Glen Aulin Trail . . . . . . . . . . . . . . . . . | 8,000 | 0.6 | 6.9 | 5.0 |
| Glen Aulin . . . . . . . . . . . . . . . . | 7,800 | 0.2 | 7.1 | 4.8 |
| *Waterwheel Falls* . . . . . . . . . . . . . . . . | 6,700 | 2.8 | | |
| Mount Conness Trail . . . . . . . . . . . . . | 8,700 | 4.0 | 11.1 | 0.8 |
| Tuolumne Meadows (Soda Springs) . | 8,600 | 0.8 | 11.9 | 0.0 |

Leaving the trail hub at Tenaya Lake, we cross the Tioga Road and go north up Murphy Creek on the McGee Lake Trail through a forested valley to a low divide. Here we come to the junction of the

*May Lake Trail* (8,700—3.0) (18b), branching west

to May Lake (3.5) and continuing south from May
Lake to the Tenaya Lake Trail (5.2). Half a mile from
our junction the Ten Lakes Trail (18) branches north
from the May Lake Trail and passes around Tuolumne
Peak to Ten Lakes (11.3) (see Sec. 7). This trail offers
the opportunity of a circuit via 18, 17, 21 and 20, via
Tuolumne Peak, Ten Lakes, and Pate Valley, returning up the Tuolumne Canyon. Passing by the trail
junction described above we continue on to

*McGee Lake* (8,100—3.3), which lies to the east of
the trail. A short distance beyond we cross a very low
divide and meet the

*Glen Aulin'-Tuolumne Canyon Trail* (21) (8,000—
0.6). From the junction it is 0.2 mile down to the High
Sierra Camp at Glen Aulin and 6.0 miles up the river
to the ranger station in Tuolumne Meadows. So we
digress from the direct route to Tuolumne Meadows
and descend to the Tuolumne River to visit Glen Aulin
and the Waterwheel Falls (camping at Lower Glen
Aulin). We cross the river to

*Glen Aulin High Sierra Camp* (7,800—0.2) (camping), ideally situated below roaring White Cascade,
with a view down the Tuolumne Canyon, through
which the trail descends to Pate Valley. Glen Aulin
and Pate Valley are starting points for trips into the
northern Yosemite National Park region (see Sec. 9).
(Limited grazing ½ mile downstream from the camp.)
The primary attraction of the region is the

*Waterwheel Falls* (6,700—2.8) below Glen Aulin.
This, with the exception of Rainbow Fall on the Middle Fork of San Joaquin River, is the most beautiful
Sierra fall outside of Yosemite Valley. The raging tor-
rent of the Tuolumne, descending a steep granite

slope, strikes a ledge, causing the water to rise high into the air in an enormous arc. Above, within a mile, are located two other large falls which are frequently mistaken for Waterwheel Falls. The Waterwheel Falls are ordinarily seen at their best in June or early July; later in the season, when the volume of water is less, they usually lack their distinctive character. Returning 3.0 miles, we pass the junction of the McGee Lake Trail (20) on our right and go up the south side of the Tuolumne River on the Glen Aulin Trail (21); later cross to the north side and continue on up the river, traversing beautiful meadows and passing the

*Mount Conness Trail* (8,700—4.0) on the left (16), by which it is 5.3 miles northeast to Young Lake (camping and grazing) and about 4 miles farther to the summit of Mount Conness. Beyond Young Lake the seldom used trail has become a ducked route and is not easy to follow. Continuing on up the river, we come to

*Tuolumne Meadows* (8,600—0.8), at Soda Springs. A mile and a quarter beyond is the ranger station.

### Sec. 4. Alternate Route No. 4

*Merced Lake and Vogelsang Pass Trail*

| *Yosemite V. to Tuolumne Meadows* | El. above Sea level | Dist. from pt. above | Dist. from Yosemite | Dist. to Tuol. Mdws. |
|---|---|---|---|---|
| Happy Isles | 4,035 | 0.0 | 0.0 | 33.5 |
| Little Yosemite (lower end) | 6,150 | 4.7 | 4.7 | 28.8 |
| Echo Creek Trail Junction | 7,000 | 6.6 | 11.3 | 22.2 |
| Merced Lake High Sierra Camp | 7,200 | 1.7 | 13.0 | 20.5 |
| Vogelsang Pass Trail (Ranger Station) | 7,300 | 0.8 | 13.8 | 19.7 |
| Babcock Lake-Tuol'ne Pass Trail | 8,200 | 1.0 | 14.8 | 18.7 |
| Isberg Pass Trail | 8,700 | 1.1 | 15.9 | 17.6 |
| Bernice Lake Trail | 9,700 | 2.9 | 18.8 | 14.7 |
| Vogelsang Pass | 10,700 | 1.3 | 20.1 | 13.4 |

| *Yosemite V. to Tuolumne Meadows* | El. above Sea level | Dist. from pt. above | Dist. from Yosemite | Dist. to Tuol. Mdws. |
|---|---|---|---|---|
| Vogelsang Lake .................. | 10,340 | 0.8 | 20.9 | 12.6 |
| Fletcher Lake (junction AR 3) | | | | |
|    Vogelsang High Sierra Camp ..... | 10,200 | 0.4 | 21.3 | 12.2 |
| Evelyn Lake ..................... | 10,330 | 1.4 | 22.7 | 10.8 |
| Ireland Lake Trail ............... | 10,400 | 2.1 | 24.8 | 8.7 |
| Lyell Fork-Muir Trail ............. | 8,800 | 2.8 | 27.6 | 5.9 |
| Tuolumne Meadows Ranger Station . | 8,700 | 5.9 | 33.5 | 0.0 |

This route is the same as the Muir Trail (see Sec. 2) from Yosemite Valley to Little Yosemite Valley. From the lower end of

*Little Yosemite Valley* (6,150—4.7) we continue to follow the Merced Lake Trail (26) up the beautiful valley, presenting pleasing vistas of forest, stream, meadow and canyon walls. Above the valley we follow the river to

*Echo Creek* (7,000—6.6) (trail junction, see Sec. 2) where is found the Aspen Glen campsite (only public grazing in this region). Proceeding, we skirt the north shore of Merced Lake to its upper end and arrive at

*Merced Lake High Sierra Camp* (7,000—1.7) (camping). Merced Lake is one of the fine glaciated lakes of the Sierra and a good day's hike from Yosemite Valley. Worthwhile side trips to equally beautiful Washburn Lake and Mt. Clark. We continue to the junction of the

*Vogelsang Pass Trail* (7,300—0.8), at Merced Lake Ranger Station (camping and grazing). The Red Peak Pass Trail continues up the canyon to Washburn Lake (7,640—2.4) and beyond (see Sec. 6B). We climb out of the canyon on the Vogelsang Pass Trail which ascends the Maclure Fork of the Merced River (Lewis Creek) and soon come to the

*Babcock Lake-Tuolumne Pass Trail* (8,200—1.0)

(AR 3, see Sec. 5). This alternate route along Fletcher Creek is shorter, but the scenery is much less spectacular than on AR 4.

We continue up Lewis Creek to its beautiful headwaters in a rocky basin, with lakes interspersed, and an imposing surrounding high mountain background. On the way we pass the junction of the

*Isberg Pass Trail* (8,700—1.1), which branches east (25) from our route (see Sec. 6).

Leaving the junction of the Isberg Pass Trail, we reach the headwaters of Lewis Creek, where a trail to Bernice Lake (camping and grazing—1 mile east) leaves our route on the right. Passing the junction of the

*Bernice Lake Trail* (9,700—2.9) we climb to the top of the ridge between Parsons Peak and Vogelsang Peak at

*Vogelsang Pass* (10,700—1.3) (fine view) and then descend to

*Vogelsang Lake* (10,340—0.8). Continuing along near timberline we come to Fletcher Creek flowing out of

*Fletcher Lake* (10,200—0.4) (camping). Here we meet the Babcock Lake-Tuolumne Pass Trail (AR 3) and nearby is the Vogelsang High Sierra Camp. From Fletcher Lake we may descend to Tuolumne Meadows on the short route by way of Rafferty Creek (see Sec. 5) or by way of lovely

*Evelyn Lake* (10,330—1.4) (camping). After passing the lake we go over a ridge (10,600) and pass the branching

*Trail to Ireland Lake* (10,400—2.1) which lies 3 miles south (camping). Descending into the canyon we meet the Muir Trail at

*Lyell Fork of the Tuolumne* (8,800—2.8) (camping) which we follow down the long valley floor to the *Tuolumne Meadows Ranger Station* (8,700—5.9).

## Sec. 5. Alternate Route No. 3

### *Merced Lake and Tuolumne Pass Trail*

| *Yosemite V. to Tuolumne Meadows* | El. above Sea level | Dist. from pt. above | Dist. from Yosemite | Dist. to Tuol. Mdws. |
|---|---|---|---|---|
| Happy Isles | 4,035 | 0.0 | 0.0 | 28.1 |
| Junction Vogelsang Pass Trail and Tuolumne Pass Trail | 8,200 | 14.8 | 14.8 | 13.3 |
| Trail to Babcock Lake | 8,800 | 1.7 | 16.5 | 11.6 |
| Trail to Emeric Lake | 9,400 | 1.9 | 18.4 | 9.7 |
| Boothe Lake Trail | 9,400 | 0.0 | 18.4 | 9.7 |
| Vogelsang High Sierra Camp Fletcher Lake (Junction AR 4) | 10,200 | 2.2 | 20.6 | 7.5 |
| Tuolumne Pass | 10,300 | 0.8 | 21.4 | 6.7 |
| Lyell Fork-Muir Trail | 8,750 | 5.0 | 26.4 | 1.7 |
| Tuolumne Meadows Ranger Station | 8,700 | 1.7 | 28.1 | 0.0 |

This route is the same as AR 4 (see Sec. 4) from Yosemite Valley to the

*Junction of Vogelsang Pass and Tuolumne Pass Trail* (8,200—14.8) on the Maclure Fork (Lewis Creek) of Merced River. Leaving the junction we descend to and cross the stream a short distance above its junction with Fletcher Creek and then ascend the canyon of Fletcher Creek through a rocky gorge, dominated by a glaciated dome, to the north of which lies Babcock Lake, and come to the junction of the

*Trail to Babcock Lake* (8,800—1.7). The lake is reached by a short scramble from our route, from which it is not visible. From the lake a tributary of Fletcher Creek hurtles down a steep granite slope in swirling cascades. Beyond the dome our trail passes through numerous meadows (fine flowers in season—

camping and grazing). East of the upper end of the last long and beautiful meadow towers Vogelsang Peak, an easy climb up a gentle slope from this point on our route. The view from this peak, owing to its position midway between the Sierra Crest and the Clark Range, is as fine as any to be found on the peaks of the Yosemite National Park. At the upper end of the meadow we come to the junction of the

*Emeric Lake Trail* (9,400—1.9) which leaves our route on the left and goes 0.4 mile west to the lake. Good campsites and grazing will be found on the western shore of the lake from whose outlet, which frames a fine view of Mt. Clark, the water flows down over granite slopes in beautiful cascades. The inlet stream, Emeric Creek, comes from Boothe Lake, which lies at the upper end of a long basin. A branching trail goes up the rocky basin, interspersed with small meadows and lakelets, to Boothe Lake (10,000—2.5) (camping), follows around the south shore of the lake (fine heather in season) and meets our trail again above the upper end of the lake just south of Tuolumne Pass.

From the trail junction we follow up Fletcher Creek, traversing the upper meadow, and then ascend a forested slope to the south end of Fletcher Lake where we meet the trail from Vogelsang Pass (AR 4, see Sec. 4). Here we find the highest of the High Sierra Camps, the

*Vogelsang Camp* (10,200—2.2). From the trail junction our route follows the west-branching trail to

*Tuolumne Pass* (10,200—0.8). From the pass we descend Rafferty Creek and meet the Muir Trail on the

*Lyell Fork of the Tuolumne* (8,750—5.0), which we follow down the meadow to

*Tuolumne Meadows Ranger Station* (8,700—1.7).

## Sec. 6. Headwaters of the Merced and Adjacent Regions

*A–Isberg Pass-Fernandez Pass Circuit (26-25-27-30)*

| Points on the Route | El. above Sea level | Dist. from pt. above | Dist. from Yosemite | Dist. to Yosemite |
|---|---|---|---|---|
| Happy Isles . . . . . . . . . . . . . . . . . . . . . . | 4,035 | 0.0 | 0.0 | 61.9 |
| Junction Isberg Pass Trail . . . . . . . . . | 8,700 | 15.9 | 15.9 | 46.0 |
| Lyell Fork Crossing . . . . . . . . . . . . . . | 9,100 | 6.0 | 21.9 | 40.0 |
| Lateral to Red Peak Pass Trail . . . . . . | 9,900 | 4.4 | 26.3 | 35.6 |
| Junction Isberg-Post Peak Trails . . . . | 10,200 | 1.2 | 27.5 | 34.4 |
| *Isberg Pass* . . . . . . . . . . . . . . . . . . . . . . | 10,500 | 0.8 | 28.3 | 35.2 |
| Post Peak Pass . . . . . . . . . . . . . . . . . . . | 10,700 | 1.4 | 28.9 | 33.0 |
| Trail to Clover Meadow . . . . . . . . . . . | 9,000 | 5.3 | 34.2 | 27.7 |
| Rutherford Lake Trail . . . . . . . . . . . . . | 9,400 | 1.2 | 35.4 | 26.5 |
| Fernandez Pass . . . . . . . . . . . . . . . . . | 10,175 | 1.0 | 36.4 | 25.5 |
| Moraine Meadow . . . . . . . . . . . . . . . . | 8,700 | 3.6 | 40.0 | 21.9 |
| Merced Pass Trail . . . . . . . . . . . . . . . . | 8,800 | 1.2 | 41.2 | 20.7 |
| Merced Pass . . . . . . . . . . . . . . . . . . . . . | 9,300 | 1.8 | 43.0 | 18.9 |
| Red Peak Pass Trail . . . . . . . . . . . . . . . | 9,000 | 1.0 | 44.0 | 17.9 |
| Junction Mono Meadow Trail . . . . . . | 6,500 | 9.4 | 53.4 | 8.5 |
| Junction Buena Vista Trail . . . . . . . . . | 6,400 | 0.1 | 53.5 | 8.4 |
| Glacier Point . . . . . . . . . . . . . . . . . . . . | 7,200 | 3.8 | 57.3 | 4.6 |
| Yosemite Village (4 Mile Trail) . . . . . | 3,970 | 4.6 | 61.9 | 0.0 |

This circuit offers many scenic attractions. Leaving Yosemite Valley on the Nevada Fall Trail and Merced Lake Trail (26), the route explores the headwaters of the Merced and some of its tributaries while encircling the Clark Range. We follow AR 4 (see Sec. 4) to the junction of the

*Isberg Pass Trail* (8,700—15.9). This trail (25) climbs up to and goes along a plateau north of the Merced River (fine view of the Clark Range and Washburn Lake). We cross the

*Lyell Fork* (9,100—6.0) (camping), which after a long beautiful cascade joins the Merced. (Before reaching the crossing a faint trail, impassable to stock,

turns off eastward through open forest to the Lyell
Fork Meadows—good camping and easy access to
climbs of Maclure, Lyell, Rodgers, Electra and Foerster peaks.) Leaving the Lyell Fork, we climb a rocky
trail up a steep sloping ledge to a bench which the trail
follows along the eastern rim of the canyon of Triple
Peak Fork of the Merced. (See Part II, Sec. 5 for
description of knapsack route to Muir Trail at
Thousand Island Lake.) Above the trail, along the
western side of the Merced-San Joaquin Divide, extending from Foerster Peak to Isberg Pass, lies a glacial basin containing several beautiful lakes, the largest
being Harriet Lake (10,300). We pass the

*Lateral to Red Peak Pass Trail* (9,900−4.4) which
descends 1.2 miles to meet that trail on Triple Peak
Fork (see Sec. 6B), and come to the

*Junction of the Isberg Pass and Post Peak Pass
Trails* (10,200−1.2). The Isberg Pass Trail turns east
and ascends to

*Isberg Pass* (10,500−0.8) on the summit of the divide which separates the watersheds of the Merced
and the San Joaquin rivers., From the divide there is a
fine view of the Clark Range to the west and of the
Cathedral Range and Merced Canyon to the north. To
the east, their base hidden by a ridge, rise Banner
Peak, Mt. Ritter, and The Minarets. The view from
Post Peak (11,009), nearby, has the advantage of
higher elevation. Descending from the pass on the San
Joaquin side is the Little Jackass Trail (WL 1),
which follows down Granite Creek to Granite Creek
Campground (WA 1) (see Part II, Secs. 12-13),
whence the Mammoth Trail (WA 2) goes to Reds
Meadow, where it joins the Muir Trail on the Middle

Fork of the San Joaquin River. This makes possible an interesting circuit returning to Yosemite on the Muir Trail from Reds Meadow via Shadow Lake, Garnet Lake and Thousand Island Lake to Donohue Pass (see Part II, Sec. 1), and thence via Tuolumne Meadows by one of the several routes described in Secs. 2, 3, 4 and 5. From Isberg Pass Junction we proceed on our circuit, ascending on the Post Peak Trail (27). Upon arriving at the crest we follow it south to cross

*Post Peak Pass* (10,700—1.4). We cross the divide and descend onto its forested southern slope, cross several tributaries of the west fork of Granite Creek branch of the Middle Fork of the San Joaquin River, and come to the junction of the

*Clover Meadow Trail* (9,000—5.3) which branches off (34) to Clover Meadow.

We now ascend, passing the junction of the

*Rutherford Lake Trail* (9,400—1.2) and cross the divide again to the Merced River watershed at

*Fernandez Pass* (10,175—1.0), where fine views are again offered. Descending we pass a lateral to Breeze Lake, which lies south half a mile, and arrive at

*Moraine Meadow* (8,700—3.6) (camping and grazing poor at campsite but good 1 mile upstream), on the South Fork of the Merced River. A trail goes up the main fork of the stream to Horse Thief Meadow at its headwaters from where Triple Divide Peak and Merced Peak may be easily climbed and marvelous views enjoyed. Near the lower end of Moraine Meadow another trail branches south to beautiful Chain Lakes (9,100—3.5). Proceeding west we come to the junction of the

*Merced Pass Trail* (8,800—1.2), leading back to

Yosemite, while the Moraine Meadow Trail continues on west toward Wawona. We ascend northerly on the Merced Pass Trail (30) to Merced Pass (9,295) and descending soon come to the junction of the

*Red Peak Trail* (9,000—2.8) (see Sec. 6B). We then descend a mile to Illilouette Creek (good camping, poor grazing), which we follow to the crossing of the Clark Fork (good camping, poor grazing). A mile beyond we come to the junction of the

*Trail to Nevada Fall* (7,000—7.8) branching northward. Here we have the choice of a route to Yosemite Valley via Nevada Fall (4.6) as an alternate. Proceeding westward on our trail we descend to Illilouette Creek where is met the

*Mono Meadow Trail* (6,500—1.6) (camping). Going northward it leads to Nevada Fall (3.9) and going westward to Mono Meadow (2.3) (good camping, poor grazing), situated ½ mile by trail below the Glacier Point Road. After crossing the stream we come to the junction of the

*Buena Vista Trail* (6,400—0.1) (31) (see Sec. 6C). We proceed on this trail down the creek, meet the Panorama Trail coming from Nevada Fall and ascend to

*Glacier Point* (7,200—3.8). From the Glacier Point Lodge we descend via the Four Mile Trail to

*Yosemite Village* (3,970—4.6).

## B–Red Peak Pass Trail (26C)

This trail follows a route outstanding in scenic beauty and provides a circuit from Yosemite via Nevada Fall and Merced Lake up the great canyon of the Merced

River, with its many cascades and waterfalls, to its headwaters. After crossing the Clark Range at Red Peak Pass with its marvelous views and descending to Ottoway Lakes, return to Yosemite may be made via Glacier Point or Nevada Fall. The distance of the round trip is about 58 miles. Leaving Yosemite Valley we follow the Merced Lake Trail to Merced Lake (see Sec. 4).

| *Merced Lake to Ottoway Lakes* | El. above Sea level | Dist. from pt. above | Total distance | |
|---|---|---|---|---|
| Merced Lake High Sierra Camp .... | 7,200 | 0.0 | 0.0 | 22.3 |
| Junction Vogelsang Pass Trail ...... | 7,300 | 0.8 | 0.8 | 21.5 |
| Washburn Lake ................... | 7,600 | 2.4 | 3.2 | 19.1 |
| Lyell Fork ....................... | 7,900 | 2.6 | 5.8 | 16.5 |
| Lateral to Isberg Pass Trail ......... | 9,100 | 4.5 | 10.3 | 12.0 |
| Red Peak Pass ................... | 11,200 | 7.0 | 17.3 | 5.0 |
| Lower Ottoway Lake ............. | 9,700 | 2.4 | 19.7 | 2.6 |
| Merced Pass Trail Junction ........ | 9,000 | 2.6 | 22.3 | 0.0 |

Leaving the *Merced Lake High Sierra Camp* (7,200—0.0) we go upstream to the junction of the

*Vogelsang Pass Trail* (7,300—0.8). Nearby is the Merced Lake Ranger Station. We proceed up the forested canyon of the Merced (some large, fine juniper trees on the north side) with frequent glimpses of the river, flanked by high canyon walls, to

*Washburn Lake* (7,600—2.4) (camping). The trail skirts the north shore of this lovely lake and then traverses the walled-in valley of the Upper Merced. Here the Lyell Fork, the Merced Peak Fork and the Triple Peak Fork drop over from three directions in dashing cascades to form the main river. We cross the river on a bridge at the

*Lyell Fork* (7,900—2.6) (good campsite and some grazing) and continue upstream to the head of the canyon, where a fine view is had of the long, beautiful cascade of Triple Peak Fork. Crossing the Merced Peak Fork, we now climb out of the canyon to the rim, where the Triple Peak Fork drops over, and follow up the forested valley of that swift-flowing stream to a junction with the

*Lateral to Isberg Pass Trail* (9,100—4.5) which branches east and ascends about one mile to meet the Isberg Pass Trail (25). The Red Peak Trail turns westward passing through a high mountain region of forest, lakes and meadows along the eastern side of the Clark Range at the headwaters of the Triple Peak Fork, Merced Peak Fork and Red Peak Fork of the Merced River. Good campsites and grazing are to be found. Our trail gradually ascends to above timberline and crosses the range on the flank of Red Peak (11,699) just south of its summit, at

*Red Peak Pass* (11,200—7.0), where we enjoy fine views, including that of Mt. Ritter and The Minarets to the east. From the pass Red Peak may be climbed to its summit, from which a marvelous sweeping view is presented. We descend on the western side of the range through a basin between Red Peak and Merced Peak containing the beautiful Ottoway Lakes and come to

*Lower Ottoway Lake* (9,700—2.4), where good camping and grazing will be found. Beyond, our trail traverses forested slopes at the headwaters of Illilouette Creek to meet the

*Merced Pass Trail* (30) (9,000—2.6) leading back to Glacier Point, Nevada Fall and Yosemite Valley. (See Sec. 6A.)

A recommended high knapsack route (no trail beyond Ostrander Lake) leading to the Red Peak Trail from Bridalveil Meadow Campground on the Glacier Point Road is via Ostrander Lake, Horse Ridge and Buena Vista Crest to the Merced Pass Trail and Red Peak Trail Junction. Distance about 16 miles.

## C–Trails from Wawona

Wawona is a starting point for trails leading to southern Yosemite National Park which connect with the park trail system.

The Alder Creek Trail (33), route of the old Indian trail to Yosemite and Mono Lake, works north, crosses the Glacier Point Road to Peregoy Meadow, and descends into Yosemite Valley on the Pohono and Glacier Point trails. By way of Glacier Point, the distance is about 26 miles.

The Chilnualna Falls Trail (32) starts its climb from the Chilnualna Road, 1.5 miles up the South Fork of the Merced River from Wawona. After climbing out of the canyon, this trail meets the Buck Camp Trail (28) which, going northward from the junction leads to Yosemite, and going eastward meets the Merced Pass Trail (30) near Moraine Meadow (see Sec. 6A). (In mid- to late summer the creeks are often dry.)

### Chilnualna Falls-Buck Camp Trail (32-38)

| Wawona to Moraine Meadow | El. above Sea level | Dist. from pt. above | Total distance | |
|---|---|---|---|---|
| Wawona ........................ | 4,000 | 0.0 | 0.0 | 20.2 |
| Chilnualna Falls Trail ............. | 4,200 | 1.5 | 1.5 | 18.7 |
| Buck Camp Trail Junction ......... | 7,800 | 6.7 | 8.2 | 12.0 |
| Buena Vista Trail Junction ........ | 8,700 | 5.0 | 13.2 | 7.0 |
| Buck Camp Ranger Station ........ | 8,250 | 1.3 | 14.5 | 5.7 |
| Merced Pass Trail Junction ........ | 8,800 | 4.5 | 19.0 | 1.2 |
| Moraine Meadow ................. | 8,700 | 1.2 | 20.2 | 0.0 |

Starting from *Wawona* (4,000—0.0) we take the road to

*Chilnualna Falls Trail* (32) (4,200—1.5). After a long climb out of the canyon of the South Fork of the Merced River, passing the Chilnualna Falls and a lateral trail (7,600—4.1) which branches north, we come to a junction with the

*Buck Camp Trail* (7,800—6.7). Northward this trail (28) goes to meet the Alder Creek Trail (33) on its way to Yosemite. A trail branching eastward goes to Ostrander Lake (3.9). Less than a mile from our junction, northward on the Buck Camp Trail, the Chilnualna Lakes Trail (29) branches eastward and follows that stream to its headwaters to meet the Buena Vista Trail (31) (9,000—5.0) between Horse Ridge and Buena Vista Peak (see below). We proceed eastward on the Buck Camp Trail, passing Grouse Lake, Crescent Lake and Johnson Lake. Good camping and grazing are to be found at all three lakes. A short distance east of Johnson Lake we come to the junction of the

*Buena Vista Trail* (8,700—5.0), referred to above. This trail (31) leads north to Yosemite, total distance about 21 miles. The trail ascends an open slope to cross a pass (9,600—2.0) over the divide just east of Buena Vista Peak (fine views, as the name implies) and then descends into a lake basin (camping and grazing) to a junction (9,000—1.0) with trail 29 branching west to the headwaters of Chilnualna Creek where lie three lakes (camping and grazing) north and west of Buena Vista Peak. From this junction the Buena Vista Trail descends to the Mono Meadow Trail junction (6,500—8.7) near Illilouette Creek. From here trails lead to Yosemite via Nevada Fall or Glacier Point, distance about 8 miles either way. Proceeding on our route we pass a lateral trail branching north via Royal Arch Lake to meet the Buena Vista Trail above the lake, and soon come to

*Buck Camp Ranger Station* (8,250—1.3) (good camping and grazing). From here we take the Moraine Meadow Trail (27), passing the junction of the Chiquito Lake Trail (1.1) which branches south to cross Chiquito Pass (8,039—3.0) and descends to meet the Forest Service road from Bass Lake in the San Joaquin watershed. Half a mile from the trail junction, a trail branches east from the Chiquito Trail to Chain Lakes (5.5) (fine camping and grazing). We continue on our route through a forested country to a junction with the

*Merced Pass Trail* (8,800—4.5). Here we have a choice of two routes, one on the Merced Pass Trail (30) (see Sec. 6B) and the other on the Fernandez Pass Trail (27) (see Sec. 6A) via

*Moraine Meadow* (8,700—1.2).

## Sec. 7. Ten Lakes and Tuolumne Canyon Trails (18-21)

Two other interesting routes from Yosemite to Tuolumne Meadows may be taken, offering a variety of scenery, including the Grand Canyon of the Tuolumne River, which is all that its name implies, with its gorges, cataracts, and waterfalls. These routes themselves provide circuits from and back to Yosemite, or they may be included in circuits taking in Tuolumne Meadows and returning to Yosemite by one of the high mountain routes, via the headwaters of the Merced River.

## Ten Lakes Trail (18)

| Yosemite V. to Tuolumne Meadows | El. above Sea level | Dist. from pt. above | Dist. from Yosemite | Dist. to Tuol. Mdws. |
|---|---|---|---|---|
| Yosemite Village | 3,970 | 0.0 | 0.0 | 40.5 |
| Top of Yosemite Falls | 6,600 | 4.0 | 4.0 | 36.5 |
| Yosemite Creek Spur Trail | 7,500 | 4.3 | 8.3 | 32.2 |
| Old Tioga Road | 7,200 | 1.8 | 10.1 | 30.4 |
| White Wolf Trail | 8,100 | 5.0 | 15.1 | 25.4 |
| Grant Lakes Trail | 9,500 | 2.8 | 17.9 | 22.6 |
| Ten Lakes | 9,200 | 1.5 | 19.4 | 21.1 |
| May Lake Trail | 8,800 | 10.8 | 30.2 | 10.3 |
| Tuolumne Meadows (via 20, 21) | 8,700 | 10.3 | 40.5 | 0.0 |

Leaving Yosemite Valley by the Yosemite Falls Trail (22), we climb the winding zigzags, getting fine intimate views of the fall, to the

*Top of Yosemite Falls* (6,600—4.0). Here we have the thrilling view of the fall and the valley from the brink of the precipice where the water leaps over, and in the distance we see the high mountain background. We continue up Yosemite Creek on the Hetch Hetchy Trail (22) through a forested section to the junction of the

*Yosemite Creek Spur Trail* (7,500—4.3). We take the Spur Trail up Yosemite Creek, and come to the

*Old Tioga Road* (7,200—1.8). Following the road a short distance east, we take the Ten Lakes Trail (18), continuing up the stream. We cross to the west bank of Yosemite Creek before crossing the new Tioga Road and continuing on to the junction of the

*White Wolf Trail* (8,100—5.0), which comes from White Wolf (17). We ascend to the headwaters of Yosemite Creek, passing the

*Grant Lakes Trail* (9,500—2.8), which branches south to the two lakes, 1.1 and 1.5 miles from our route. We then cross the divide (9,700) separating the headwaters of Yosemite Creek from the Tuolumne. From the summit a ridge leads north about 1.5 miles to Colby Mountain (9,631), occupying a commanding position on the rim of the Grand Canyon of the Tuolumne and rising 4,700 feet in elevation above the Muir Gorge. From its summit, easily reached from this point, there is a marvelous view of the canyon. From the divide we descend to

*Ten Lakes* (9,200—1.5), reposing in a basin on the canyon rim which drains into the Tuolumne. (Fine camping and grazing.) Our trail goes eastward across Ten Lakes Basin to the rim of the canyon of the south fork of Cathedral Creek, and then south up the canyon, which it crosses, and then works around the north and east slope of Tuolumne Peak coming to the junction of the

*May Lake Trail* (8,800—10.8). Southward the May Lake Trail (18b) goes via May Lake 9.8 miles to meet the Tenaya Lake Trail (AR 1, see Sec. 3) below the Tioga Road, offering that route of return to Yosemite. Proceeding northward on our way to Tuolumne Meadows, we descend to and follow the McGee Lake and Glen Aulin trails (20-21, see Sec. 3) to

*Tuolumne Meadows Ranger Station* (8,700—10.3).

## *Tuolumne Canyon Trail (21)*

| *Yosemite V. to Tuolumne Meadows* | El. above Sea level | Dist. from pt. above | Dist. from Yosemite | Dist. to Tuol. Mdws. |
|---|---|---|---|---|
| Yosemite Village ................. | 3,970 | 0.0 | 0.0 | 44.4 |
| Junction Yosemite Creek Spur ..... | 7,500 | 8.3 | 8.3 | 36.1 |
| Lukens Lake Trail ................ | 7,900 | 1.2 | 9.5 | 34.9 |
| Old Tioga Road .................. | 8,100 | 0.8 | 10.3 | 34.1 |
| White Wolf Trail................. | 8,000 | 2.3 | 12.6 | 31.8 |
| Pate Valley Trail ................ | 7,500 | 4.3 | 16.9 | 27.5 |

| _Yosemite V. to Tuolumne Meadows_ | El. above Sea level | Dist. from pt. above | Dist. from Yosemite | Dist. to Tuol. Mdws. |
|---|---|---|---|---|
| Pate Valley ...................... | 4,400 | 6.2 | 23.1 | 21.3 |
| Muir Gorge ...................... | 5,000 | 4.4 | 27.5 | 16.9 |
| Waterwheel Falls ................. | 6,700 | 7.1 | 34.6 | 9.8 |
| Glen Aulin (High Sierra Camp) ..... | 7,800 | 2.8 | 37.4 | 7.0 |
| Tuolumne Meadows Ranger Station . | 8,700 | 7.0 | 44.4 | 0.0 |

Our route leaving Yosemite is the same as that for Ten Lakes to the

_Junction of the Yosemite Creek Spur_ (7,500—8.3). From the junction we continue on the Hetch Hetchy Trail (22) to the old Tioga Road and junction of the

_Lukens Lake Trail_ (8,100—2.0). The Hetch Hetchy Trail leads to Hetch Hetchy and Mather via the old Tioga Road and the Hetch Hetchy-Harden Lake Trail (10). The distance to Hetch Hetchy from this point is about 20 miles.

We take the Lukens Lake Trail (15), pass Lukens Lake (1.5) and come to the

_White Wolf Trail_ (8,000—2.3), which we follow (17) west and then north to the junction of the

_Pate Valley Trail_ (21) (7,500—4.3) coming from the old Tioga Road and Mather. We go down the Pate Valley Trail (21) and descend into the Grand Canyon of the Tuolumne, crossing the river to the north side at

_Pate Valley_ (4,400—6.2) (camping, grazing fair early, poor later). The valley floor is thickly forested with many large oaks, and is somewhat dusty and dry in the summer season. This is a starting-point for trails leading into the Yosemite National Park region lying north of the Tuolumne. (See Sec. 9.)

From Pate Valley we travel up the canyon on the north side of the river for several miles (the trail is sometimes flooded in the spring run-off). As we approach

*Muir Gorge* (5,000—4.4) the trail mounts above the gorge, where the river roars its way through the deep chasm. (At low water it is possible to pass through the Muir Gorge by swimming the pools; but this should not be attempted except under experienced leadership.)

Descending to the river again, we continue up the canyon to

*Waterwheel Falls* (6,700—7.1), and then on to

*Glen Aulin High Sierra Camp* (7,800—2.8), whence we may return to Yosemite Valley on the McGee Lake-Tenaya Lake route (see Sec. 3), or proceed on the Glen Aulin Trail to

*Tuolumne Meadows* (8,700—7.0).

One should visit the Tuolumne Canyon as early in the summer as possible when the river is running bank full from the melting snows and the falls and cascades are at their best.

### Sec. 8. Tuolumne Meadows

The Tioga Road passes through the meadows, rendering them accessible by automobile from Highway 395 on the east side of the range via Tioga Pass; from Yosemite Valley via Crane Flat; and from the west via Big Oak Flat Road (Highway 120) and Crane Flat.

*Accommodations:* Meals and lodging may be had at Tuolumne Meadows Lodge (8,600), which is situated on the Dana Fork of the Tuolumne at the end of a side road (1.2) branching from the highway beyond the north end of the Tuolumne River bridge. The lodge opens as early as snow conditions permit, usually about June 20, and closes about Sept. 15. Showers are available. Extensive auto campgrounds will be found south of the road near the river bridge, and backpack campgrounds are a mile downstream on the north side at Soda Springs.

*Supplies:* Provisions and other supplies may be purchased at the store which is situated on the highway near the bridge. There is also a post office.

*Packers:* Packers, guides, and animals are available at the stables at Tuolumne Meadows. Address correspondence to Reservation Office, Yosemite Park and Curry Co., Yosemite Valley, California. Animals are not allowed out overnight unless a guide is taken.

At Tuolumne Meadows we find ourselves in a wide expanse of mountain meadows with forested slopes of timber stretching from the borders to an imposing high mountain background. Through this most beautiful of all High Sierra meadows peacefully meanders the Tuolumne River, contrasting strikingly with its subsequent wild and tumultuous descent through the Tuolumne Canyon and Muir Gorge.

The graceful spires of Cathedral Peak and Unicorn Peak tower above the lower end of the Meadows. The upper end is dominated by Lembert Dome in the foreground, and, in the distance, by the reddish summits of Mt. Gibbs and Mt. Dana. Between the main crest of the Sierra and the Lyell Fork Canyon, rises the massive Kuna Crest to an elevation of over 12,200 feet, forming the east wall of the canyon. At the head of the canyon rise Mt. Lyell (13,114) and Mt. Maclure with their glaciers. Tuolumne Meadows delighted

John Muir. They are especially beautiful early in the season, about July 15, when the grass is fresh and green.

## Interesting Side Trips

The Muir Trail traverses the Meadows, and laterals from the Meadows to other points offer many pleasing circuits both north and south of the Tuolumne River.

Numerous beautiful and interesting one-day side trips may be made from the Meadows, of which the following are particularly recommended:

*Dog Lake:* By trail from Tioga Pass or trail head on Tioga Road.

*Gaylor Lakes:* By trail from Ranger Station at Tioga Pass.

*Lyell Base Camp:* By Muir Trail to head of Lyell Fork of the Tuolumne.

*Young Lake and Mt. Conness* (12,590): Fine view and Conness glacier. Two routes: By trail 16 via Soda Springs, or via Dog Lake Trail, passing through beautiful woods and meadows, blooming with abundant mountain flowers in season.

*Saddlebag Lake:* Road leads to it from Tioga Road just east of the summit of Tioga Pass. Short trail to summit of Mt. Conness.

*Evelyn Lake and Ireland Lake:* By Lyell Fork and Evelyn Lake Trail.

*Elizabeth Lake:* By trail from public camp.

*Cathedral Peak* (10,940): Difficult mountain climb. Some airy places to pass. Should only be attempted by or with experienced rock-climbers.

*Mt. Dana* (13,053) *and Mt. Gibbs* (12,764): By

Tioga Road and Mono Pass Trail (23). Easy to climb. Extensive view of the crest and Mono Lake. No trail.

*Mt. Lyell* (13,095) *and glacier:* By Lyell Fork Trail (Muir Trail). Grand view. Not difficult to climb if right route is taken. Inexperienced climbers should have a guide or experienced companion.

*Lambert Dome:* By Dog Lake Trail. Fine view.

## Sec. 9. Northern Tributaries of the Tuolumne

### *Approaches Western Side*

1. From Yosemite Valley: (1) Via Tenaya Lake, McGee Lake, and Glen Aulin (see Sec. 3). (2) Via Pate Valley (see Sec. 7).

2. From Tuolumne Meadows: Via Glen Aulin.

3. From Mather: Via Hetch Hetchy Dam or Pate Valley.

4. From points on the old Tioga Road via Pate Valley.

5. From Kennedy Meadow via Relief Reservoir, meeting trail 2 at Bond Pass, distance 18 miles. Kennedy Meadow, reached by the Sonora Pass Road, is 8 miles west of Sonora Pass. (Supplies, stock, and guides.)

### *Approaches Eastern Side*

1. *Virginia Lakes Camp* (9,700): Reached by auto about 6 miles west of Highway 395. Road leaves highway at Conway Summit. Accommodations, supplies, saddle and pack stock, guides. Trail leads over pass via Summit Lake (10,200—4.0), meeting trail 14 in Virginia Canyon.

2. *Green Lake Resort* (8,200): Reached by auto from Highway 395. Road leaves highway about 4 miles south of Bridgeport. It is about 8 miles to the resort from the junction. Accommodations, supplies, pack stock, guides. From Green Lake a trail goes via Hoover and Summit lakes (10,200—5.5) and a knapsack route goes over Virginia Pass (10,500—4.0) to meet trail 14 in Virginia Canyon.

3. *Twin Lakes:* Reached by auto from Highway 395 on road leaving Bridgeport, distance 12 miles. Accommodations, supplies, saddle and pack stock. The lakes below Sawtooth Ridge afford fine views and rugged scenery. A trail follows up Robinson Creek to meet trail 6 between Snow and Crown lakes.

4. *Bridgeport:* Hotels, supplies, stock, guides. A trail turns off from Twin Lakes Road to Big Meadow (7,600—12.0) on Buckeye Creek. The Bridgeport Trail goes up Buckeye Creek over Buckeye Pass (9,600—10.0) to meet the Kerrick Canyon Trail (5).

5. *Leavitt Meadows:* On Sonora Pass Road about 7 miles west of junction with Highway 395. Public campsites; pack stock available. The Walker River Trail ascends West Walker River. Near Fremont Lake the trail forks. One goes over to the West Fork, which is then followed to its head, crosses the Sierra Crest at Emigrant Pass and meets the Relief Valley Trail from Kennedy Meadow going south to Bond Pass. The other trail continues up the main stream of West Walker River and goes over the Sierra Crest to Dorothy Lake, where it meets the Jack Main Canyon Trail (2). From Piute Meadows one trail crosses over to meet the Emigrant Pass Trail; another crosses Kirkwood Pass to Buckeye Creek.

This area north of the Tuolumne Canyon is not so rich in high mountain scenery as the regions farther south; but there is compensation in its many beautiful meadows, flowers, forests, streams, and lakes. There is good fishing in most of the lakes and streams. It is a delightful country in which to roam and to camp, especially attractive now since it is so little used and uncrowded compared to the southern Sierra.

This region is glaciated country, in shape a giant amphitheater thirty miles in width, sloping toward the Tuolumne. This was formerly a great glacier bed. Watercourses have cut its surface into many parallel canyons which drain to the southwest, and finally drop into the great canyon of the Tuolumne. Winding through the labyrinths of these canyons and over divides separating them, there is a system of trails, some of them not too well defined, which gives access to many of the lakes and points of interest in the area.

Starting from Glen Aulin, Pate Valley, or Hetch Hetchy Dam, several circuits may be made, among which the following are recommended.

(*Note:* For brevity, trail numbers are here substituted for the trail names. See index of trails).

*Circuit A: 14, 13, 11, 7, 5, 8, 12, 11, 21.*
*From Glen Aulin to Benson Lake, returning*
*via Bear Valley and Tuolumne Canyon*

| Points on the Route | El. above Sea level | Dist. from pt. above | Total distance | |
|---|---|---|---|---|
| From Glen Aulin (on 14) . . . . . . . . . . . | 7,800 | 0.0 | 0.0 | 67.7 |
| Junction 14 and 13 (Virginia Can.) . . . | 8,600 | 8.1 | 8.1 | 59.6 |
| Miller Lake (13) . . . . . . . . . . . . . . . . . . | 9,500 | 3.7 | 11.8 | 55.9 |
| Junction 13 and 6 (Matterhorn Can.) . | 8,500 | 2.2 | 14.0 | 53.7 |
| Benson Pass (13) . . . . . . . . . . . . . . . . | 10,100 | 4.4 | 18.4 | 49.3 |

| Points on the Route | El. above Sea level | Dist. from pt. above | Total distance | |
|---|---|---|---|---|
| Smedberg Lake ................... | 9,200 | 2.2 | 20.6 | 47.1 |
| Rodgers Lake (11) ............... | 9,500 | 2.4 | 23.0 | 44.7 |
| Neall Lake (11) .................... | 9,200 | 1.0 | 24.0 | 43.7 |
| Junction 11 and 7 ................ | 9,600 | 1.9 | 25.9 | 41.8 |
| Benson Lake (7) ................... | 7,600 | 3.2 | 29.1 | 38.6 |
| Junction 7 and 5 (Kerrick Can.) ..... | 8,900 | 3.5 | 32.6 | 35.1 |
| Junction 5 and 8 (via 5) ............. | 8,000 | 3.6 | 36.2 | 31.5 |
| Bear Valley (8) .................... | 9,200 | 3.0 | 39.2 | 28.5 |
| Junction 8 and 12 ................ | 8,000 | 4.5 | 43.7 | 24.0 |
| Pleasant Valley (12) .............. | 7,000 | 2.0 | 45.7 | 22.0 |
| Junction 12 and 11 ............... | 7,800 | 3.2 | 48.9 | 18.8 |
| Pate Valley (via 11) Junc. 11 and 21 .. | 4,400 | 4.9 | 53.8 | 13.9 |
| Glen Aulin (via 21, Tuolumne Can.) . | 7,800 | 13.9 | 67.7 | 0.0 |

Circuit A may also be started from Pate Valley.

### *Circuit B: 14, 13, 6, 5, 7, 11, 12, 11, 21.*
### *From Glen Aulin to the Sierra Crest via Matterhorn Canyon and Burro Pass, returning via Kerrick Canyon, Benson Lake and Tuolumne Canyon*

| Points on the Route | El. above Sea level | Dist. from pt. above | Total distance | |
|---|---|---|---|---|
| From Glen Aulin (on 14 and 13, same as A) to .................... | 7,800 | 0.0 | 0.0 | 68.2 |
| Junction 13 and 6 (Matterhorn Can.) . | 8,500 | 14.0 | 14.0 | 54.2 |
| Burro Pass (6) .................... | 10,700 | 7.0 | 21.0 | 47.2 |
| Snow Lake Pass (Sierra Crest) ...... | 10,200 | 6.0 | 27.0 | 41.2 |
| Junction 6 and 5 (Kerrick Meadow) (2 mi. to Peeler Lake) ............ | 9,300 | 3.0 | 30.0 | 38.2 |
| Junction 5 and 7 (via 5) Kerrick Can. . | 8,900 | 5.0 | 35.0 | 33.2 |
| Benson Lake (7) ................... | 7,600 | 3.5 | 38.5 | 29.7 |
| Junction 7 and 11 (Smedbg. L. 1 mi.) . | 9,600 | 3.2 | 41.7 | 26.5 |
| Rodgers Lake (11) ................. | 9,500 | 1.3 | 43.0 | 25.2 |
| Neall Lake (via 11) ................. | 9,200 | 1.0 | 44.0 | 24.2 |
| Junction 12 and 11 (via 11) .......... | 7,800 | 5.4 | 49.4 | 18.8 |
| Pate Valley (via 11) Junction 11 and 21 ................. | 4,400 | 4.9 | 54.3 | 13.9 |
| Glen Aulin (via 21, Tuolumne Can.) . | 7,800 | 13.9 | 68.2 | 0.0 |

Circuit B may also be started from Pate Valley.

The Sierra Crest, in the region of Sawtooth Ridge and Matterhorn Peak (12,264), near Burro Pass, has an alpine ruggedness and elevation not to be found any farther north in the Sierra Nevada. Here six glaciers lie on the eastern side of the crest.

### Circuit C: 11, 7, 5, 4, 2, 3, 4, 9, 12, 11.
### From Pate Valley to Tilden Lake via Benson Lake, returning via Lake Vernon and Rancheria Mountain

| Points on the Route | El. above Sea level | Dist. from pt. above | Total distance | |
|---|---|---|---|---|
| From Pate Valley (on 11) .......... | 4,400 | 0.0 | 0.0 | 77.1 |
| Junction 11 and 12 ................ | 7,800 | 4.9 | 4.9 | 72.2 |
| Junction 11 and 7 (via 11) .......... | 8,800 | 4.8 | 9.7 | 67.4 |
| Neall Lake (via 11) ................ | 9,200 | 0.6 | 10.3 | 66.8 |
| Rodgers Lake (via 11) ............. | 9,500 | 1.0 | 11.3 | 65.8 |
| Junction 11 and 7 (Smedbg. L. 1 mi.) . | 9,600 | 1.3 | 12.6 | 64.5 |
| Benson Lake (7) .................. | 7,600 | 3.2 | 15.8 | 61.3 |
| Junction 7 and 5 (Kerrick Can.) ..... | 8,900 | 3.5 | 19.3 | 57.8 |
| Junction 5 and 4 (Tilden Can.) (5) (0.2 mi. to Wilmer Lake) ........ | 8,400 | 9.4 | 28.7 | 48.4 |
| Tilden Lake (4) ................... | 8,850 | 3.1 | 31.8 | 45.3 |
| Junction Tilden L. Trail and 2 ....... | 8,100 | 2.3 | 34.1 | 43.0 |
| Wilmer Lake (2) .................. | 7,950 | 1.9 | 36.0 | 41.1 |
| Junction 2 and 3 ................. | 6,900 | 9.9 | 45.9 | 31.2 |
| Lake Vernon (3) .................. | 6,500 | 2.0 | 47.9 | 29.2 |
| Tiltill Valley (Junction 3 and 4) ...... | 5,600 | 6.8 | 54.7 | 22.4 |
| Junction 3 and 9 (Rancheria Cr.) .... | 4,600 | 2.7 | 57.4 | 19.7 |
| Junction 9 and 12 (via 9) ........... | 8,000 | 10.0 | 67.4 | 9.7 |
| Pate Valley (via 12 and 11) ........ | 4,400 | 9.7 | 77.1 | 0.0 |

Circuit C may also be taken by starting or ending at Hetch Hetchy Dam on the Lake Eleanor Road and taking 2 to Junction 2 and 3, distance 7.6 miles. The total distance of the circuit is thereby shortened to 54 miles.

### Circuit D: 11, 7, 5, 4, 2, 1.
#### From Pate Valley to Bond Pass via Benson Lake and Tilden Lake, returning via Huckleberry Lake, Kibbie Lake and Lake Eleanor

| Points on the Route | El. above Sea level | Dist. from pt. above | Total distance | |
|---|---|---|---|---|
| From Pate Valley (via 11, 7, 5, and 4, same route as Circuit C) to ....... | 4,400 | 0.0 | 0.0 | 85.2 |
| Junction Tilden Lake Trail and 2 .... | 8,100 | 34.1 | 34.1 | 51.1 |
| Junction Trail to Dorothy Lake (2) .. | 9,400 | 6.4 | 40.5 | 44.7 |
| Bond Pass (Junction 2 and 1)........ | 9,700 | 0.6 | 41.1 | 44.1 |
| Maxwell Lake Trail (via 1) (16 miles to Kennedy Meadow) ... | 8,450 | 5.4 | 46.5 | 38.7 |
| *Huckleberry Lake (1) (2.5 mi. to Twin Lakes) .......... | 7,900 | 3.5 | 50.0 | 35.2 |
| Junction Trail to Kibbie Lake ....... | 6,500 | 15.4 | 65.4 | 19.8 |
| Kibbie Lake ..................... | 6,500 | 3.0 | 68.4 | 16.8 |
| Lake Eleanor .................... | 4,650 | 7.3 | 75.7 | 9.5 |
| Hetch Hetchy Dam ............... | 3,814 | 9.5 | 85.2 | 0.0 |

Circuit D may also be taken by starting from Hetch Hetchy on the Lake Eleanor Road to its junction with 2, distance 3 miles.

*A short distance west of Huckleberry Lake a short-cut trail to Kibbie Lake leaves 1 and is about 6 miles shorter than the Forest Service Trail which follows Kibbie Ridge.

### Circuit E: Lake Eleanor Road, 2 and 1.
#### From Hetch Hetchy to Bond Pass via Jack Main Canyon, and Tilden Lake, returning via Huckleberry Lake and Lake Eleanor

| Points on the Route | El. above Sea level | Dist. from pt. above | Total distance | |
|---|---|---|---|---|
| Hetch Hetchy Dam ............... | 3,814 | 0.0 | 0.0 | 73.0 |
| Junction Lake Eleanor Road and 2 .. | 5,000 | 3.0 | 3.0 | 70.0 |
| Beehive (1.2 mi. to Laurel Lake) .... | 6,500 | 3.3 | 6.3 | 66.7 |
| Junction with 3 (Lake Vernon 1.8 mi.) | 6,900 | 1.3 | 7.6 | 65.4 |
| Wilmer Lake (Jack Main Canyon) ... | 7,950 | 9.9 | 17.5 | 55.5 |

| Points on the Route | El. above Sea level | Dist. from pt. above | Total distance | |
|---|---|---|---|---|
| Junction Tilden Lake Trail . . . . . . . . | 8,100 | 1.9 | 19.4 | 53.6 |
| Tilden Lake (and return to 2) . . . . . . . | 8,850 | 4.6 | 24.0 | 49.0 |
| Hetch Hetchy Dam (via 2, Bond Pass, 1 and Lake Eleanor Road) . . . | 3,796 | 49.0 | 73.0 | 0.0 |

## Sec. 10. The John Muir Trail

### *Tuolumne Meadows to Donohue Pass*

| Points on the Route | El. above Sea level | Dist. from pt. above | Dist. from Tuolumne Meadows | Dist. to Donohue Pass |
|---|---|---|---|---|
| Tuolumne Meadows Ranger Station . | 8,700 | 0.0 | 0.0 | 12.8 |
| Dana Fork-Parker Pass Trail . . . . . . . | 8,700 | 0.8 | 0.8 | 12.0 |
| Tuolumne Pass Trail (Rafferty Creek) . . . . . . . . . . . . . . . | 8,750 | 0.9 | 1.7 | 11.1 |
| Vogelsang Pass Trail (Evelyn Lake) . . . . . . . . . . . . . . . . . | 8,800 | 4.2 | 5.9 | 6.9 |
| Lyell Base Camp . . . . . . . . . . . . . . . . | 9,000 | 3.0 | 8.9 | 3.9 |
| Donohue Pass . . . . . . . . . . . . . . . . . . | 11,050 | 3.9 | 12.8 | 0.0 |

From

*Tuolumne Meadows Ranger Station* (8,700—0.0) we take the trail leading to the crossing of the Dana and Lyell Forks of the Tuolumne near Tuolumne Meadows Lodge, and then proceed on the Lyell Fork Trail up the beautiful, level, meadowed and forested floor of the Lyell Fork Canyon for a distance of 8 miles, keeping on the west side of the stream all the way. Shortly beyond the ranger station we pass the junction of the

*Dana Fork-Parker Pass Trail* (8,700—0.8) (AR 2, see Sec. 11) which goes up the Dana Fork of the Tuolumne. After crossing the Lyell Fork we pass the junction of the

*Tuolumne Pass Trail* (8,750—0.9) which goes up Rafferty Creek and later that of the

*Vogelsang Pass Trail* (8,800—4.2) (AR 4), both of which leave our route leading back to Yosemite by way of the Vogelsang High Sierra Camp (see Secs. 4 and 5) and the headwaters of the Merced River, scenically one of the finest regions in the Yosemite National Park. We continue up the Lyell Fork of the Tuolumne River to the

*Lyell Base Camp* (9,000—3.0), where the long flat area of the Lyell Fork Canyon terminates abruptly. There are fine campsites and grazing almost everywhere in this canyon as far as the base camp. Beyond the base camp we ascend a steep cliff and continue ascending rapidly to Donohue Pass on the Sierra Crest. This portion of the route is superb. Admirable views are enjoyed of Mt. Lyell and its glacier, which is the second largest residual glacier in California south of Mt. Shasta. After ascending the steep cliff above the base camp, we arrive at a wooded stretch at some distance to the right of the Lyell Fork to which we now return and ford to the east bank just below its junction with the Maclure Fork. We come back to the west bank of the infant Lyell Fork in a beautiful little meadow some distance above, and then continue up the now bare rocky canyon and ford a small tributary stream which descends the steep cliff above and west of the trail. This stream rises a short distance beyond the cliff in several small lakes under the Lyell and Maclure glaciers, and is a recommended route of return from the summit of Mt. Lyell. The finest intimate view of Mt. Lyell is to be had from these lakes. We continue up the canyon to the point where it turns abruptly to the southwest and offers an impressive view of the enormous amphitheater formed by Mts.

Lyell and Maclure and their perpetual glaciers. This is the point for leaving the trail to make the ascent of Mt. Lyell. Here the trail fords the headwaters of the Lyell Fork, below a small lake, and ascends a steep granite slope to the crest of the Sierra at

*Donohue Pass* (11,050—3.9). From the summit one enjoys a sweeping panorama of high mountain scenery, from Mt. Conness on the north to the Ritter Group on the south.

## Sec. 11. Alternate Route No. 2

### *Dana Fork-Parker Pass Trails*

| Tuolumne Meadows to Muir Trail at Rush Creek via Gem Lake | El. above Sea level | Dist. from pt. above | Dist. from Tuolumne Meadows | Dist. from Rush Cr. Junction |
|---|---|---|---|---|
| Tuolumne Meadows Ranger Station . | 8,700 | 0.0 | 0.0 | 24.6 |
| Dana Fork Trail . . . . . . . . . . . . . . . . . | 8,700 | 0.8 | 0.8 | 23.8 |
| Gaylor Lakes Trail  . . . . . . . . . . . . . . | 9,200 | 1.7 | 2.5 | 22.1 |
| Dana Meadows (Mono Pass Trail) . . | 9,700 | 3.4 | 5.9 | 18.7 |
| Parker Pass Trail (junction) . . . . . . . . | 10,100 | 2.0 | 7.9 | 16.7 |
| Lateral to Mono Pass Trail . . . . . . . . . | 10,700 | 2.1 | 10.0 | 14.6 |
| Parker Pass . . . . . . . . . . . . . . . . . . . . . | 11,100 | 1.0 | 11.0 | 13.6 |
| Koip Peak Pass . . . . . . . . . . . . . . . . . . | 12,350 | 3.1 | 14.1 | 10.5 |
| Alger Lake (Lower end) . . . . . . . . . . . | 10,600 | 3.0 | 17.1 | 7.5 |
| Gem Pass . . . . . . . . . . . . . . . . . . . . . . | 10,500 | 1.5 | 18.6 | 6.0 |
| Gem Lake (trail junction) . . . . . . . . . | 9,100 | 2.0 | 20.6 | 4.0 |
| Rush Creek (trail junction) . . . . . . . . . | 9,200 | 0.8 | 21.4 | 3.2 |
| Muir Trail (Rush Creek Crossing) . . . | 9,600 | 3.2 | 24.6 | 0.0 |

This is a good alternate route which may be taken south from Tuolumne Meadows instead of the heavily traveled section of Muir Trail up the Lyell Fork. It meets the Muir Trail between Donohue Pass and Island Pass at Rush Creek. This route traverses a high, rugged region along the Sierra Crest and offers unusually fine and sweeping views. From

*Tuolumne Meadows Ranger Station* (8,700—0.0)

we start on the Muir Trail (Sec. 10) to the junction of the

*Trail up Dana Fork* (8,700—0.8) (no camping allowed in entire Dana Fork watershed) which branches east after we cross that stream. We follow up the south bank and later cross to the north side where the

*Gaylor Lakes Trail* (9,200—1.7) branches northward to Gaylor Lakes (3.3). Our trail follows between the stream and the Tioga Road to

*Dana Meadows* (9,700—3.4) (a Tioga Road trail head) where we follow the Mono Pass Trail south along the west side of the Sierra Crest and ascend up Parker Pass Creek between Mt. Gibbs and the Kuna Crest to the

*Junction of Mono Pass and Parker Pass Trails* (10,100—2.0). Here the Mono Pass Trail (23) turns eastward to cross Mono Pass (10,604) nearby, and then descends Bloody Canyon (here known as the Mono Lake Trail, being the old Indian trail from Mono Lake) to Walker Lake (7,935—5.1) where is met a road to Highway 395 and Mono Lake. The Parker Pass Trail (24) proceeds south to cross the crest at

*Parker Pass* (11,100—3.1) and then works southward along its eastern side at the headwaters of Parker Creek, which is crossed (10,900) (possible campsite for hikers only). The trail now climbs a steep wall by switchbacks and then turns toward the crest above and south of the Koip Peak Glacier to cross

*Koip Peak Pass* (12,350—3.1). The pass is over a saddle between Koip Peak (12,979) and Parker Peak (12,861), but not over the Sierra Crest. The views along this section of the trail are marvelous. From the summit of Koip Peak (one-half mile to the west and easily climbed from the pass) the panorama is spectacular. Northward the view extends along the crest to the Matterhorn Peaks. Southward the Ritter Range with its glaciers is completely open to view, and the crest can be seen down to the region of Mt. Abbot. Westward, beyond the great canyon of the Lyell Fork, rises the Cathedral Range, and eastward are marvelous views over the Mono Basin to Nevada and across Owens Valley to the White Mountains. From the pass the trail descends steeply into the basin of

*Alger Lake* (10,600—3.0) with its wild and impressive surroundings. (Fine campsites and some grazing at lower end of the lake.) From the lake we ascend to

*Gem Pass* (10,500—1.5) and then descend to the

*Gem Lake Trail Junction* (9,100—2.0) at the north end of the lake. (See Part II, Secs. 3 and 4.) We proceed along the west side of Gem Lake (reservoir) to Rush Creek. Here the Gem Lake Trail crosses the stream and ascends to Agnew Pass, but we turn west up Rush Creek, pass to the north of Waugh Lake (reservoir), and meet the

*Muir Trail* (9,600—4.0) near the Rush Creek crossing.

# PART II:
# Middle Fork of San Joaquin River Region

The Sierra Crest is indented on its eastern side in the vicinity of Mt. Lyell by the drainage basin of Rush Creek. Here the crest swings southwestward from Koip Crest to Mt. Lyell and the Muir Trail crosses at Donohue Pass. The crest then swings eastward to San Joaquin Mountain, from where it resumes its normal trend. The Muir Trail crosses at Island Pass. The short portion of the route between Donohue Pass and Island Pass is the only region where the Muir Trail traverses the eastern side of the Sierra.

To the south, the Middle Fork of the San Joaquin River and its main tributary, Fish Creek, flow from opposite directions for some distance parallel to and near the main crest until they turn and converge before entering the South Fork. The crest of the range in this region appears to have been cut away. Extending southward from Mt. Davis is a high rugged spur separating the Middle Fork from the North Fork of the San Joaquin. Along its crest rise Banner Peak, Mt. Ritter, and The Minarets, with beautiful lakes on their eastern slopes. The scenic attractions and alpine summits of this region are found here rather than on the main crest. Southward from Shadow Lake, the region traversed by the Muir Trail lacks the grandeur of other parts of the route until Silver Pass is approached, although several points of interest, such as Devils Postpile and Rainbow Fall, are passed on the way.

### Sec. 1. The John Muir Trail

#### Donohue Pass to Silver Pass

| Points on Route | El. above Sea level | Dist. from pt. above | Dist. from Don. Pass | Dist. from Silver Pass |
|---|---|---|---|---|
| Donohue Pass ................... | 11,050 | 0.0 | 0.0 | 43.2 |
| Rush Creek Trail ................ | 9,600 | 3.1 | 3.1 | 40.1 |

| Points on Route | El. above Sea level | Dist. from pt. above | Dist. from Don. Pass | Dist. from Silver Pass |
|---|---|---|---|---|
| Island Pass ...................... | 10,250 | 1.2 | 4.3 | 38.9 |
| Thousand Island Lake (east end) .... | 9,850 | 2.0 | 6.3 | 36.9 |
| Garnet Lake ..................... | 9,700 | 1.7 | 8.0 | 35.2 |
| Shadow Creek Trail ............... | 9,200 | 2.9 | 10.9 | 32.3 |
| Shadow Lake (upper end) .......... | 8,750 | 1.1 | 12.0 | 31.2 |
| Rosalie Lake ..................... | 9,500 | 1.5 | 13.5 | 29.7 |
| Gladys Lake ..................... | 9,600 | 0.7 | 14.2 | 29.0 |
| Johnston Lake—Minaret Creek Trail | 8,150 | 3.5 | 17.7 | 25.5 |
| Mammoth Trail ................... | 7,550 | 1.8 | 19.5 | 23.7 |
| Middle Fork San Joaquin River ..... | 7,500 | 0.2 | 19.7 | 23.5 |
| Devils Postpile ................... | 7,550 | 0.2 | 19.9 | 23.3 |
| Reds Meadow .................... | 7,600 | 0.7 | 20.6 | 22.6 |
| Mammoth Pass Trail junction ...... | 8,700 | 1.4 | 22.0 | 21.2 |
| Lateral to Mammoth Pass Trail ..... | 8,900 | 1.3 | 23.3 | 19.9 |
| Junction Red Cones Trail .......... | 8,700 | 0.2 | 23.5 | 19.7 |
| Lateral to Mammoth Pass Trail ..... | 8,900 | 0.9 | 24.4 | 18.8 |
| Deer Creek (Mammoth Crest Rt.)... | 9,200 | 2.0 | 26.4 | 16.8 |
| Duck Lake Trail .................. | 10,100 | 5.2 | 31.6 | 11.6 |
| Purple Lake ..................... | 9,900 | 2.4 | 34.0 | 9.2 |
| Lake Virginia ................... | 10,300 | 1.7 | 35.7 | 7.5 |
| McGee Pass Trail (Tully Hole) ..... | 9,500 | 2.0 | 37.7 | 5.5 |
| Cascade Valley (Fish Creek Trail) .. | 9,100 | 1.2 | 38.9 | 4.3 |
| Goodale Pass Trail ............... | 10,300 | 2.7 | 41.6 | 1.6 |
| Silver Pass...................... | 10,900 | 1.6 | 43.2 | 0.0 |

## From

*Donohue Pass* (11,050—0.0) on the crest we rapidly descend into the headwaters of Rush Creek, following down a small tributary to its junction with the main stream. Here the country is forested (camping and grazing—spectacular high mountain surroundings). We cross two forks of the stream. Here we come to the junction of the

*Rush Creek Trail* (9,600—3.1) (EL 1, see Secs. 3 and 4), which comes from Silver Lake and Gem Lake. After leaving Rush Creek we ascend a low divide to

*Island Pass* (10,250—1.2). The Sierra Crest south of Island Pass surrenders its alpine summits and scenic attractions to the Ritter Range, whose peaks rise two to three thousand feet higher to the west. The Ritter Range is a remnant of an ancient mountain system and, as François Matthes writes, "when you climb Mount Ritter you climb the core of one of the ancestral mountains that were formed more than a hundred million years before the present Sierra Nevada was uplifted."

Geologically the Ritter Range is composed of dark mottled rocks representing ancient lavas, highly metamorphosed, associated with a complex of dark igneous rocks. This tough rock has resisted the forces of erosion through the ages, which accounts for the height of the range. The joint planes generally are vertical, or at high angles, with northwesterly trends. This structure causes the almost vertical faces and knife-edge ridges which are characteristic of the range. Caution is called for in climbing because of the danger of loose blocks or slabs which may pull away from the faces. Returning to the western watershed, we descend an easy slope to the headwaters of the Middle Fork of the San Joaquin River at

*Thousand Island Lake* (9,850—2.0), which the trail strikes near its eastern end. This lake, dotted with rocky islets, with its grassy shores, fine flowers in season, and its rugged, barren surroundings, is one of the grandest sights of the Sierra. The commanding massif of Banner Peak dominates the scene at the upper end of the lake. The mightier Mt. Ritter from here resembles an insignificant spur extending from Banner's left. (Camping and grazing around and below the lake after the snow leaves.)

The trail crosses the outlet stream near the lower end, from which point there is a fine panorama of high

mountain scenery extending from Lyell to Banner. Here is a junction with two trails. One goes down the canyon of the Middle Fork of the San Joaquin River, following the river much of the way, to Agnew Meadows (8,335—6.8) (see Sec. 6). Trails branch to Garnet Lake, Agnew Pass and Shadow Lake (see Sec. 5). The other skirts around the northern end of the canyon, crosses the Sierra Crest (8,300) near Agnew Pass and meets the Agnew Pass Trail near Clark Lakes on the east side. (See Sec. 5.)

Few regions in the Sierra vie in scenic magnificence with the region in the vicinity of Ediza, Shadow, Garnet, and Thousand Island lakes, Mt. Ritter, Banner Peak, and The Minarets.

At the lower end of Thousand Island Lake we ford its outlet and ascend southward to the pass between Garnet and Thousand Island lakes (10,200) on the top of a low dividing ridge between the two lakes, from which we descend to the

*Northern Shore of Garnet Lake* (9,700—1.7) at a point near its eastern end on a recently made trail. This is a long desolate lake with rocky islets and grassy shores, very sparsely wooded. The sheer wall of Banner Peak rises directly above its upper end; cliffs of red, black, and silver rock flank its two sides; and a low gap at the outlet affords a charming vista into the canyon of the San Joaquin. (Good grazing around lake; best camping, rather exposed, on south side just beyond place where the trail leaves the lake for Shadow Creek—timber rather scarce.) We proceed to the east end of the lake where a branching trail descends to the San Joaquin River Trail (see Sec. 5). We now skirt the south shore for half a mile and then as-

cend to the pass between Shadow Lake and Garnet
Lake (10,000) on the top of a steep dividing ridge. Intimate views of Mt. Ritter and its glacier and an interesting view southward are enjoyed from the top of
the ridge. From here a steep descent is made to
Shadow Creek. The view of The Minarets, enjoyed
from several points on the way down, is one of the
grandest sights in the Sierra. This group is a tremendous wall of sheer rock, with numerous jagged spires
and pinnacles crowning its crest and dazzling small
glaciers reposing beneath. We reach the forested floor
of the beautiful valley of Shadow Creek near a delightful meadow where we strike the

*Trail along the North Bank of Shadow Creek*
(9,200—2.9). This meadow (fine camping and view of
Ritter and Banner), and the less attractive one immediately below, afford the nearest good feed for
stock while camping at Shadow Lake. The trail we
strike comes up Shadow Creek from the Middle Fork
of the San Joaquin River and, from our junction with it
at the meadow above Shadow Lake, continues up
Shadow Creek. It crosses several pleasing meadows
(offering fine views of The Minarets, camping and
grazing), and fords branches of the stream several
times before ending at Lake Ediza about 2 miles above
the junction of the trail to Thousand Island Lake. Lake
Ediza, in its spectacular place at the headwaters of
Shadow Creek and set in the giant crown of Ritter,
Banner, and The Minarets, is one of the brightest gems
in the Sierra. Mt. Ritter (13,157) is the highest peak
north of Mt. Abbot, and with its sister peak, Banner,
constitutes one of the noblest groups in the entire
range. These peaks can be climbed from Lake Ediza
by any fairly experienced climber.

About 1½ miles south of Lake Ediza lie Iceberg Lakes (10,100–10,350) in a wild setting at the very foot of The Minarets. Ice often remains on these lakes until late in summer, hence the name.

From the trail junction a well-traveled trail goes down the north bank of Shadow Creek, skirts the north shore of Shadow Lake, and continues on to Agnew Meadows (see Sec. 7). We proceed on this trail to the

*Upper End of Shadow Lake* (8,750—1.1). There are several ready-made camp spots here (usually populated—better to camp up the creek) and very poor grazing.

From the upper end of Shadow Lake the Muir Trail crosses to the south side of Shadow Creek above the lake's inlet and skirts the lake to its south shore. Here we leave the lake and climb southward up a steep grade through forest to the plateau above, where we arrive at

*Rosalie Lake* (9,500—1.5). Proceeding around the east side of the lake, we cross its outlet and ascend southward through wooded country until we top a rise beyond which is

*Gladys Lake* (9,600—0.7). We pass west of this quiet little lake, descend gradually through forests and continue south through a meadowy country, finally leaving the plateau to descend to

*Johnston Lake* (8,150—3.5) and its surrounding meadows. Here we meet the Minaret Creek Trail. This trail, rough in places, leads up Minaret Creek to beautiful Minaret Lake (10,000—4.0). This is another route of approach to Iceberg Lakes and The Minarets, whose spires tower above the lake. The Muir Trail turns down Minaret Creek on the south side, past a west-branching trail leading to the Beck Lakes and later striking the

*Mammoth Trail* (7,550—1.8) from Soldier Meadow (Sec. 13) (WL 2) shortly before we reach the

*Middle Fork of the San Joaquin River* (7,500—0.2). On the east side of the stream, which we cross on a bridge, is the junction with the trail leading north to the road end at Devils Postpile Ranger Station.

The Muir Trail turns south downstream a short distance to the famous

*Devils Postpile* (7,550—0.2), a cliff, facing the river, composed of peculiar postlike formations of columnar basalt, reminding one of a honeycomb, with a mass of broken columns beneath it. Be sure to look at the top of the postpile as well as the usual view from the side.

The Devils Postpile is a national monument under the basic jurisdiction of the National Park Service.

We leave the stream and soon arrive at

*Reds Meadow* (7,600—0.7) (good camping and grazing—small enclosed tourist pasture; hot springs and public baths).

From Reds Meadow a detour of about 2 miles takes us down the river to Rainbow Fall, the trail leading to the cliffs above the river from which the best view of the fall may be enjoyed. The trail continues down the cliff and ends at the river. One can work up the river to the base of the fall. I think Rainbow Fall is the most beautiful in the Sierra outside of Yosemite Valley. The full volume of the Middle Fork of the San Joaquin plunges over the cliff into a misty sunlit pool at its base, where the rainbow forms. Although not notable for its height, the fall resembles Yosemite's Vernal Fall, being perfectly formed in an ideal setting.

The Muir Trail parallels the Reds Meadow road to its end, circles around behind the Reds Meadow Pack Station, then climbs up the east side of the valley. The trail turns south on a level bench passing the

*Mammoth Pass Trail Junction* (8,700—1.4) where that trail turns off and continues to climb over the crest to Mammoth Lakes. The Muir Trail continues south along the sloping bench, passing the junction (8,900—0.2) of the Red Cones Trail which descends by a different route to the campgrounds at Reds Meadow (see Sec. 6). Beyond, another lateral leading to Mammoth Pass branches from our trail (8,900—0.9). We soon enter the John Muir Wilderness of the Sierra and Inyo National Forests, crossing the divide separating the watersheds of Fish Creek and the main San Joaquin Middle Fork (9,200) and gradually ascending in a southeasterly direction along the rim of the canyon of Fish Creek to

*Deer Creek* (9,200—2.0) where a route (trail not maintained, often difficult to find) follows up the creek to Deer Lakes (10,500—3.5). From here a well-maintained trail climbs to Mammoth Crest (11,200—0.6) which is followed northwestward (magnificent sweeping views) for nearly 3 miles until it drops down to the end of the Mammoth Lakes Road at Lake George. Total distance about 9 miles. (See Sec. 9.)

Our trail continues along the rim of the canyon of Fish Creek to the crossing of the stream coming from Duck Lake. Beyond we come to the junction of the

*Duck Lake Trail* (10,000—5.2) (EL 4, see Sec. 9). The Muir Trail ascends around the point of a ridge and then drops down to

*Purple Lake* (9,900—2.4) (camping, good grazing).

From the outlet of the lake a trail goes down the canyon wall to Cascade Valley to meet the Fish Creek Trail (8,400—2.4) (see Sec. 2).

Our trail crosses a divide to

*Lake Virginia* (10,300—1.7) (camping, grazing). After skirting the east side of the lake, it descends at Tully Hole to the headwaters of Fish Creek which flows down from a chain of lakes, lying in a high granite basin, above which rise to the east Red Slate Mountain (13,163) and Red-and-White Mountain (12,850).

At Tully Hole (good grazing) on Fish Creek we meet a trail coming down the north bank of the stream from the Sierra Crest. This is the

*McGee Pass Trail* (9,500—2.0) (EL 5, see Sec. 11). Fish Creek turns sharply to the southwest just above the point where our trail descends, and we follow down the gorge to the forks at the

*Head of Cascade Valley* (9,100—1.2), where we cross and meet the old route of the Muir Trail coming up from Cascade Valley, the Crater Creek-Fish Creek Trail (AR 5, see Sec. 2).

We follow up a tributary stream, fording near its forks, and go up the north side of the east fork (crossing several small meadows—camping and grazing) to a lake basin containing five lakes, the lower one being Lake of the Lone Indian. Our trail continues up the east branch of this drainage, fords the creek at the outlet of Squaw Lake (formerly Helen Lake), and crosses the basin to the west branch of the drainage and the north shore of Chief Lake (formerly Warrior Lake). Before reaching Chief Lake the

*Goodale Pass Trail* (10,300—2.7) branches westward, fords the outlet of Papoose Lake and climbs steeply to Goodale Pass, whence it descends steeply via Graveyard Meadows to WL No. 3 (see Part III, Sec. 11) at Lake Thomas Edison (7,600—7.5). The Muir Trail ascends between Chief Lake and Warrior Lake (formerly Bobs Lake) and crosses the Silver Divide at

*Silver Pass* (10,900—1.6) from which a fine view is enjoyed of Mt. Ritter and Banner Peak far to the northwest.

### Sec. 2. Alternate Route No. 5

*Crater Creek-Fish Creek Trail*

| Reds Meadow to Silver Pass | El. above Sea level | Dist. from pt. above | Total distance | |
|---|---|---|---|---|
| Reds Meadow.................... | 7,600 | 0.0 | 0.0 | 24.5 |
| Crater Creek Crossing ............ | 6,800 | 5.0 | 5.0 | 19.5 |
| Rim of Fish Valley ................ | 7,050 | 3.0 | 8.0 | 16.5 |
| Fish Creek Crossing .............. | 6,400 | 2.0 | 10.0 | 14.5 |
| Fish Creek Hot Springs............ | 7,200 | 3.0 | 13.0 | 11.5 |
| Cascade Valley .................. | 8,200 | 5.0 | 18.0 | 6.5 |
| Head of Cascade Valley (Muir Trail) | 9,100 | 3.5 | 21.5 | 3.0 |
| Silver Pass (Via Muir Trail) ........ | 10,900 | 3.0 | 24.5 | 0.0 |

From

*Reds Meadow* (7,600—0.0) go south on the Reds Meadow Road, past the turnoff to the Reds Meadow Campground. About one half mile farther, turn right on a spur road and follow it to the end. The trail goes south from here, soon passing a trail branching right to Rainbow Fall (see Sec. 1, p. 82). Beyond this point is a rocky ridge, to the west of which lies the deep impassable gorge of the San Joaquin and to the east of which runs Crater Creek. Our trail turns left, southeast, away from the river, passing through sandy forested stretches to Crater Creek. We soon drop down a steep pumice slope to the west bank of Crater Creek, along which we descend for some distance to the

*Crater Creek Crossing* (6,800—5.0). Fording and leaving Crater Creek, we proceed, without losing altitude, around the east wall of the canyon of the Middle Fork to the

*Rim of Fish Valley* (7,050—3.0). After descending into Fish Valley, a deep thickly forested valley with high Yosemite-like cliffs, our trail follows up the north bank of Fish Creek about one quarter mile and then crosses to the opposite bank over a steel bridge. Another quarter mile beyond, a right-branching trail (37) leads up the south wall of the valley and proceeds via Silver Creek to Huntington Lake (see Part III, Sec. 13). A lateral branches up Silver Creek to the beautiful Margaret Lakes. (No trail extends down Fish Creek.)

Our route continues straight ahead (easterly), up and around a delightful, large open meadow (only good grazing in Fish Valley) on our left, to the vicinity of the

*Old Fish Creek Crossing* (6,400—2.0). Good camp spots in this spacious valley are scarce. There are ready-made sites near the ford. About five minutes below the ford, along the trail down the south bank, there is a clean and pretty campsite next to the stream at the upper end of the meadow previously skirted (plenty of timber and fine view of cliffs above). Another campsite is at the lower (west) edge of the meadow. Fish Valley deserves its name. I have never known a day's fishing there that did not provide a limit of good-sized trout.

Our route goes up the south bank of Fish Creek on the wide level valley floor. Soon the stream forks, the valley becomes narrower and the floor rises. We ascend through boggy, brushy country to

*Fish Creek Hot Springs* (7,200—3.0), near which there is a ready-made campsite and a small meadow. Here the trail leaves the south branch and climbs around a dividing point (short steep pull) and drops into the north branch, which it later fords to the north bank. About three and a half miles above this ford, an old trail fords the river and goes up Minnow Creek to its headwater lakes. It then crosses over a divide to Lake of the Lone Indian.

Continuing up Fish Creek we come to the meadows of

*Cascade Valley* (8,200—5.0). This beautiful green spot provides the best camping and grazing on Fish Creek. (Trail to Purple Lake, Sec. 1.)

We continue up the north bank of Fish Creek and come to another large green meadow (camping and grazing). The trail later fords to the south bank of the stream and the valley floor becomes rougher and steeper. We ascend to the head of Cascade Valley where we meet the

*Muir Trail* (9,100—3.5), which is followed to

*Silver Pass* (10,900—3.0). (See Sec. 1.)

### Sec. 3. Eastern Approach No. 1

*Silver Lake*
*(Inyo National Forest:*
*Grant, Silver, Gull, and June Lakes)*

*Reached by auto:* On the June Lake Loop Road, which leaves Highway 395 five miles south of Lee Vining. The road circles past Grant, Silver, Gull, and June Lakes and then rejoins Highway 395.

*Reached by bus:* Daily on Highway 395 between Los Angeles and Reno.

*Accommodations:* Hotels and resorts at Silver Lake and June Lake. Also at Lee Vining and Mono Lake, where the Tioga Road, coming from Tuolumne Meadows, meets the highway.

*Supplies:* Stores at each place.

*Saddle and pack stock and guides:* Silver Lake.

*Silver Lake, Gull Lake, June Lake* and *Grant Lake* lie in a long valley, slightly above the elevation of Mono Basin, at the foot of the eastern slope of the range. The trip to the summit of

*San Joaquin Mountain* is the most popular one-day excursion. The peak is very easy of ascent and commands one of the finest views of the Mammoth region (Mt. Ritter, Banner Peak, The Minarets) seen across the Middle Fork of the San Joaquin River.

Excursions may be made over Agnew Pass to Shadow Lake and Thousand Island Lake and to the Middle Fork of the San Joaquin. Starting from Silver Lake, the Rush Creek Trail connects with the Parker Pass Trail (see Sec. 4) and Agnew Pass Trail (see Sec. 5) and finally meets the Muir Trail near its crossing of Rush Creek.

## Sec. 4. Eastern Lateral No. 1

### *Rush Creek Trail*

| *Silver Lake to Muir Trail* | El. above Sea level | Dist. from pt. above | Total distance | |
|---|---|---|---|---|
| Silver Lake (north end) ............ | 7,223 | 0.0 | 0.0 | 8.0 |
| Agnew Pass Trail (Agnew Lake) .... | 8,500 | 2.0 | 2.0 | 6.0 |
| Parker Pass Trail (Gem Lake) ...... | 9,100 | 2.0 | 4.0 | 4.0 |
| Rush Creek ...................... | 9,200 | 0.8 | 4.8 | 3.2 |
| Muir Trail (Rush Creek Crossing) ... | 9,600 | 3.2 | 8.0 | 0.0 |

This lateral to the Muir Trail starts at the northern end of

*Silver Lake* (7,223—0.0), works southward up the cliff above the lake, crosses the Southern California Edison Company's cable-car tracks, and continues upward to Agnew Lake. Here the

*Trail to Agnew Pass* (8,500—2.0) (see Sec. 5) branches south, crosses the stream on a good bridge below the Agnew Lake Dam, and climbs to the pass (9,950—2.5).

The Rush Creek Trail ascends on the north side of Agnew Lake and Gem Lake to meet the

*Parker Pass Trail* (9,100—2.0) (see below) above the northern end of Gem Lake. Here we turn south and follow the trail to

*Rush Creek* (9,200—0.8). The Rush Creek Trail branches west, following up the north bank of the stream and passing around the north side of Waugh Lake (a reservoir which has been made by flooding Rush Meadow), and then continues up Rush Creek to meet the

*Muir Trail* (9,600—3.2) between Donohue Pass and Island Pass—the only spot where the Muir Trail traverses the eastern side of the Sierra Crest. (Good camping and grazing is available in the upper Rush Creek region—though for some reason it's always windy here.)

## Parker Pass Trail

Just above Gem Lake the Parker Pass Trail (24) comes in from Tuolumne Meadows. This route turns south at Dana Meadows near Tioga Pass on the Mono Pass

Trail (23), and follows down the west side of the crest to Mono Pass. Here the trail branches. One branch (23) goes over the pass and down Bloody Canyon to Walker Lake, where it meets a road to Highway 395. The other (24) proceeds south, crosses the Sierra Crest at Parker Pass and continues along the eastern side of the crest past Alger Lake to Gem Lake. From Tuolumne Meadows to Gem Lake the distance is about 21 miles (see Part I, Sec. 11 for description of this trail).

### Sec. 5. Eastern Lateral No. 2

#### *Agnew Pass Trail*

| *Silver Lake to Agnew Meadows, Shadow Lake and Thousand Island Lake* | Elev. above Sea level | Dist. from point above | Total distance |
|---|---|---|---|
| Silver Lake ...................... | 7,223 | 0.0 | 0.0 |
| Agnew Lake (trail junction) ........ | 8,500 | 2.0 | 2.0 |
| Agnew Pass ...................... | 9,950 | 3.0 | 5.0 |
| Trail Junction .................... | 9,500 | 1.0 | 6.0 |
| *(a) Agnew Meadows* | | | |
| (The High Trail) .............. | 8,300 | 5.3 | 11.3 |
| *(b) Muir Trail—Garnet Lake* ...... | 9,700 | 2.2 | 8.2 |
| *Muir Trail—Shadow Lake* ..... | 8,750 | 4.5 | 10.5 |
| *(c) Muir Trail—* | | | |
| *Thousand Island Lake* .......... | 9,850 | 2.0 | 8.0 |

From

*Silver Lake* (7,223—0.0) we climb to the foot of

*Agnew Lake* (8,500—2.0). Here the Agnew Pass Trail heads south, crossing Rush Creek on the bridge below the Agnew Lake Dam. We zigzag up a rocky slope to Spooky Meadows, which is nestled in a cirque of red and black lava cliffs marking the end of the San Joaquin Mountain ridge, and then continue on to the

Clark Lakes. After passing the lower Clark Lake, we turn left on a short-cut trail to

*Agnew Pass* (9,950—3.0). The pass overlooks the vast canyon of the Middle Fork of the San Joaquin River from its northern rim (view southward as far as Seven Gables). A short steep descent from the pass (another little lake, quite picturesque) brings you to the head of the valley, and to the intersection with a

*Trail Junction* (9,500—0.1). Here three trails branch.

(a) The Agnew Meadows Trail (known as the High Trail) goes south along the east rim of the canyon to *Agnew Meadows* (8,300—5.3) (see Sec. 6), offering fine views of the Ritter Range along the way.

(b) A trail descends to the river where it meets the San Joaquin River Trail (8,900—1.0) coming down the eastern side of the stream from Thousand Island Lake. Downstream, from the last junction, it is about 2 miles to the Shadow Lake Trail (see Sec. 7) which ascends to the lake where it meets the Muir Trail beyond the upper end of *Shadow Lake* (8,750—3.5). Upstream from the junction, a branching trail ascends to meet the Muir Trail at *Garnet Lake* (9,700—1.2).

From the Shadow Lake Trail junction, the San Joaquin River Trail (see Sec. 7) goes along the eastern side of Olaine Lake and continues down the valley, past the turnoff to Agnew Meadows, and on to Devils Postpile, the distance from Agnew Pass being about 10 miles.

(c) A trail goes west across the head of the canyon, joins the San Joaquin River Trail and meets the Muir Trail at the lower end of *Thousand Island Lake* (9,850—2.0).

## Sec. 6. Eastern Approach No. 2

*Mammoth Lakes*
*(Inyo National Forest)*

*Reached by auto:* On road which leaves Highway 395 about 30 miles south of Mono Lake, passing Mammoth Visitor Center (3.0), Post Office and Store, to Lake Mary (8.0), ending at Horseshoe Lake.

*Reached by bus:* Daily from Los Angeles and Reno.

*Airport:* 10 mi. south of Mammoth Lakes with daily flights from Los Angeles.

*Accommodations:* Resorts at Mammoth Lakes and Reds Meadow.

*Supplies:* Stores at Mammoth Lakes, Twin Lakes, Lake Mary, Lake Mamie, and Reds Meadow.

*Saddle and pack stock, guides:* Mammoth Lakes, Agnew Meadows, Reds Meadow.

About one mile west of the *Mammoth Visitor Center* (7,900) a road branches north from the Mammoth Lakes highway to

*Minaret Summit* (9,175—6.0), passing the misnamed "Earthquake Fault," a deep, long, remarkably well-defined crack in the lava rock. Minaret Summit is the pass over the Sierra Crest and is situated on the eastern rim of the canyon of the Middle Fork of San Joaquin River, a short distance north of Mammoth Lakes. There is an impressive and sweeping view of the valley of the upper San Joaquin, Banner Peak, Mt. Ritter, and The Minarets. The road descends into the San Joaquin Canyon and branches about 1.5 miles below the summit. One branch continues to

*Agnew Meadows,* which is located on a bench above the river (good grazing and camping), 2.5 miles from

Minaret Summit and 8.5 miles from the Mammoth Visitor Center. This is the most convenient starting point for Shadow Lake, Ritter, and Banner, and points north on the Muir Trail (see Sec. 7).

The left-hand branch of the road turns back down the canyon and descends to the river at Pumice Flat, and continues down the river to

*Reds Meadow,* 6.7 miles from the summit and 12.7 miles from Mammoth Ranger Station.

At *Mammoth Lakes* (8,900) there are nineteen lakes within a five-mile radius of Lake Mary, the largest of the group. Several attractive lodges are located at the lakes, and there are extensive public campgrounds.

The Mammoth Lakes area is one of the most popular playgrounds of the eastern Sierra region. The many lakes and the beautiful woods, in their rugged, colorful, semi-circular mountain background, make the region very attractive.

Side trips to Devils Postpile, Rainbow Fall, "Earthquake Fault," Minaret Summit, and Duck Lake are recommended. The beautiful back country—Cascade Valley, Minaret, Shadow, Ediza, Garnet, and Thousand Island Lakes, and the upper Rush Creek region—is easily accessible.

## Sec. 7. Agnew Meadows

### Shadow Creek Trail

| *Agnew Meadows to Lake Ediza* | El. above Sea level | Dist. from pt. above | Dist. from Agnew M. | Dist. to L. Ediza |
|---|---|---|---|---|
| Agnew Meadows . . . . . . . . . . . . . . . . . | 8,300 | 0.0 | 0.0 | 6.3 |
| San Joaquin River Trail . . . . . . . . . . . | 8,100 | 1.3 | 1.3 | 5.0 |
| Shadow Creek Trail . . . . . . . . . . . . . . | 8,100 | 1.3 | 2.6 | 3.7 |
| Lower End of Shadow Lake . . . . . . . . | 8,750 | 0.7 | 3.3 | 3.0 |

| *Agnew Meadows to Lake Ediza* | El. above Sea level | Dist. from pt. above | Dist. from Agnew M. | Dist. to L. Ediza |
|---|---|---|---|---|
| Upper End of Shadow Lake, Muir Trail | 8,750 | 0.7 | 4.0 | 2.3 |
| Lake Ediza | 9,300 | 2.2 | 6.2 | 0.0 |

From

*Agnew Meadows* (8,300—0.0) the trail descends into the canyon of the Middle Fork of the San Joaquin River where it meets the

*San Joaquin River Trail* (8,100—1.3) coming from Thousand Island Lake.

Our route follows this trail northward and when approaching the river passes Olaine Lake in a meadow to the west of the trail which affords good camping and grazing. On the east bank of the river we come to the junction of the

*Shadow Creek Trail* (8,100—1.3) which fords the infant San Joaquin and climbs up the rough, steep wall of the canyon to the immediate right of Shadow Creek Falls. After passing through a narrow rocky gap we arrive at the

*Lower End of Shadow Lake* (8,750—0.7). The view up the lake from a point across the outlet toward Ritter and Banner is very beautiful. Campsites are overused and rather exposed to wind. Our trail skirts the steep north shore of the lake to the

*Upper End of Shadow Lake* (8,750—0.7) where we meet the Muir Trail coming down Shadow Creek (see Sec. 1). There are several ready-made camping spots here (usually populated) and very poor grazing. Better grazing and camping will be found less than a mile upstream. We now follow the Muir Trail up Shadow Creek to its junction with our trail and then continue on to

*Lake Ediza* (9,300—2.2). (See pages 79 to 80 for a description.)

## Sec. 8. Eastern Lateral No. 3

### *Mammoth Pass Trail*
### *Mammoth Lakes to Muir Trail*

From the end of the Mammoth Lakes Road at Horse-shoe Lake (8,960) the Mammoth Pass Trail ascends westward to McLeod (McCloud on U.S.G.S.) Lake where the trail forks on Mammoth Pass (9,300—1.0). The south-branching trail descends from the pass and then turns southward along the slope of the range where it forks. The right-branching trail meets the Muir Trail near the Red Cones (8,900—2.0), and the left-branching trail continues along the slope to meet the Muir Trail farther south (8,900—3.5). The trail branching north at Mammoth Pass descends to meet the Muir Trail (8,700—1.5) about a mile and a half from Reds Meadow (see page 82).

## Sec. 9. Eastern Lateral No. 4

### *Duck Lake Trail*

This trail starts from the end of the road at the southern end of Lake Mary (8,900—0.0) and follows up the chain of lakes skirting Arrowhead Lake and Skelton Lake, passing along the shore of Barney Lake and over Duck Pass (10,800) on the Sierra Crest to Duck Lake (10,427—6.0). This beautiful lake is just over the summit. High cliffs surround it and a vista of distant peaks is framed in the gap at its lower end. The trail skirts the west side of the lake and descends below it to meet the Muir Trail on the north rim of the canyon of Fish Creek.

### Eastern Lateral No. 4B

#### *Mammoth Crest Route*

From the end of the road near Lake George (9,008) a trail ascends steeply to the Sierra Crest, here known as Mammoth Crest (10,400—2.0). This spectacular trail follows the crest southwestward for about 3 miles (fine, sweeping views) reaching an elevation of 11,200 before turning down the south side of the crest to Deer Lakes (10,500—3.5). From Deer Lakes a trail follows Deer Creek downstream to meet the Muir Trail. Or from the upper Deer Lake, a route goes through the low gap to the east to meet the Duck Lake Trail, which is followed to the Muir Trail.

### Sec. 10. Eastern Approach No. 3

#### *Long Valley*

Several approaches may be taken from Long Valley, which extends along the upper reaches of the Owens River. A crucial approach road leads away from the Sierra 3 miles east to Hot Creek hot springs, an active geothermal area where many new eruptions of hot water have surfaced in the last two years.

A short lateral road leaves Highway 395 about five miles south of Mammoth and leads two miles to Convict Lake (7,580) (pack station, store). The lake has rugged mountain surroundings, made interesting by the highly colored rock structure. A trail ascends

Convict Creek for several miles to lakes at its headwaters, the largest being Lake Dorothy and Lake
Genevieve.

From McGee Creek Resort, on the highway 4 miles
south of the Convict Lake Road and about 33 miles
north of Bishop, a road ascends McGee Creek 3.5
miles to the McGee Creek Pack Station (see Sec. 11).
From here a trail crosses McGee Pass to the head of
Fish Creek.

Going south on the highway less than 2 miles from
McGee Creek, a short road turns up Hilton Creek.
From here a trail ascends Hilton Creek to the Hilton
Lakes. Davis Lake is the largest of the group. These
lakes lie under the main crest below Mt. Stanford and
Mt. Huntington. A lateral trail crosses the divide from
the Hilton Lakes to Rock Creek Lake (EA 4, see Part
III, Sec. 2).

## Sec. 11. Eastern Lateral No. 5

### McGee Pass Trail

| McGee Creek to Muir Trail at Fish Creek | El. above Sea level | Dist. from pt. above | Dist. from McGee C. | Dist. to Tully H. |
|---|---|---|---|---|
| McGee Creek Pack Station ........ | 7,700 | 0.0 | 0.0 | 13.0 |
| Big McGee Lake ................. | 10,500 | 6.5 | 6.5 | 6.5 |
| McGee (Red Slate) Pass ........... | 11,900 | 2.0 | 8.5 | 4.5 |
| Muir Trail at Tully Hole ........... | 9,500 | 4.5 | 13.0 | 0.0 |

From *McGee Creek Pack Station* (7,700—0.0) the
McGee Pass Trail follows a mining road about 4 miles
and then continues up the northwest bank of the
stream for another 3 miles to
*Big McGee Lake* (10,500—6.5), a very beautiful
campsite. From the lake a trail works northward up
the basin on the east side of the tributary stream and

the highest large lake. At the upper end of the basin, above the lake, a craggy defile opens ahead, colorful and spectacular, up which the trail leads to

*McGee (Red Slate) Pass* (11,900—2.0). From the pass the trail descends the open grassy basin from level to level over airy, sky-parlor meadows to the head of Fish Creek. After fording several times, the trail follows down the stream and descends into the canyon called Tully Hole at the lower end of which is met the

*Muir Trail* (9,500—4.5) (see Sec. 1). The McGee Pass Trail explores a region rich in scenic grandeur, and is the best approach for climbing Red Slate Mountain, Red-and-White Mountain and Mt. Stanford.

## Sec. 12. Western Approach No. 1

*Granite Creek Campground*
*(Sierra National Forest;*
*Granite Creek Fork of San Joaquin River)*

*Reached by auto:* From Frenso or Madera via Bass Lake (distance about 85 miles); via North Fork (distance about 95 miles).

*Accommodations:* Bass Lake, public camps and resorts; North Fork, motel.

*Supplies:* Bass Lake, North Fork.

*Saddle and pack stock:* At Miller Meadow, near end of the road.

From Granite Creek Campground several trails radiate. The San Joaquin River Trail (36) proceeds south, crosses the Middle Fork on the Miller Bridge, and follows up the east side of the South Fork of the San Joaquin to Mono Creek (WA 2, see Part III, Sec.

10). A branching trail (37) leads to Fish Valley and AR 5 via Silver Creek (see Part III, Sec. 13).

## Western Lateral No. 1

### *Granite Creek Campground to Isberg Pass*

From Granite Creek Campground (7,000) the Little Jackass Trail (WL 1) ascends to the headwaters of the East Fork of Granite Creek, passing the Cora Lakes (8,400—5.0) and Sadler Lake (9,345—10.0) (camping and grazing), and meets the Isberg Pass Trail (25) on Isberg Pass (10,500—12.0) (see Part I, Sec. 6A).

## Sec. 13. Western Lateral No. 2

### *Mammoth Trail*

| Soldier Meadow to Devils Postpile | El. above Sea level | Dist. from pt. above | Total distance | |
|---|---|---|---|---|
| Soldier Meadow | 7,000 | 0.0 | 0.0 | 18.8 |
| Sheep Crossing (N. F. San Joaquin R.) | 6,100 | 5.0 | 5.0 | 13.8 |
| Summit Meadow | 9,000 | 9.0 | 14.0 | 4.8 |
| King Creek Crossing | 7,600 | 2.4 | 16.4 | 2.4 |
| Muir Trail (Devils Postpile) | 7,550 | 2.4 | 18.8 | 0.0 |

The Mammoth Trail to Devils Postpile traverses a rough country on the north side of the great canyon of the Middle Fork of the San Joaquin River. Leaving
*Soldier Meadow* (7,000), the trail crosses a low divide (7,600) and then makes a long descent into the canyon of the North Fork of the San Joaquin, crossing the river at
*Sheep Crossing* (6,100—5.0) whence a steady climb of 2 miles is made up the north canyon wall to Snake Meadow (7,100). (One mile beyond Sheep Crossing, the Junction Butte Trail goes south to the junction of

the Middle and North Forks of the San Joaquin River.) At Snake Meadow a trail branches north to the headwaters of the North Fork of the San Joaquin River. The climb continues 2.6 miles to Cargyle Meadow (8,000) (camping and grazing) and on up the Granite Stairway to

*Summit Meadow* (9,000—9.0). Here a trail branches north to the headwaters of King Creek at Beck Lakes (9,850—4.0) which lie south of The Minarets. A lateral goes to Lake Ashley (9,600—3.5) at the foot of Iron Mountain (11,149). Our trail descends into Snow Canyon and crosses

*King Creek* (7,600—2.4), follows down the north bank for a mile and then turns northward up the valley of the Middle Fork of the San Joaquin River. Before crossing the east bank on a bridge we meet the Muir Trail coming from Johnston Lake (see Sec. 1). We cross the stream and go downstream a short distance to

*Devils Postpile* (7,550—2.4).

# PART III:
# South Fork of San Joaquin River Region

**and North Fork of Kings River**

After descending from Silver Pass, the Muir Trail follows a course somewhat away from the Sierra Crest, traveling through forested valleys contrasted with cascading streams and open meadows. Upon reaching Evolution Valley we again find the more rugged grandeur of the high country near the crest.

## Sec. 1. The John Muir Trail

### *Silver Pass to Muir Pass*

| *Points on the Route* | El. above Sea level | Dist. from pt. above | Dist. from Silver Pass | Dist. to Muir Pass |
|---|---|---|---|---|
| Silver Pass | 10,900 | 0.0 | 0.0 | 47.8 |
| Silver Pass Lake | 10,350 | 0.6 | 0.6 | 47.2 |
| North Fork of Mono Creek | 8,900 | 3.0 | 3.6 | 44.2 |
| Mono Pass Trail | 8,300 | 1.4 | 5.0 | 42.8 |
| Mono Creek Bridge | 7,700 | 1.6 | 6.6 | 41.2 |
| Bear Ridge | 9,950 | 4.6 | 11.2 | 36.6 |
| Bear Creek | 8,800 | 2.1 | 13.3 | 34.5 |
| Hilgard Branch—Lake Italy Trail | 9,250 | 2.3 | 15.6 | 32.2 |
| East Fork of Bear Creek Lakes Trail | 9,500 | 1.2 | 16.8 | 31.0 |
| Marie Lake | 10,600 | 2.6 | 19.4 | 28.4 |
| Selden Pass | 10,872 | 1.3 | 20.7 | 27.1 |
| Heart Lake | 10,490 | 0.7 | 21.4 | 26.4 |
| Sally Keyes Lakes | 10,200 | 0.8 | 22.2 | 25.6 |
| Trail to Blayney Meadows | 10,100 | 0.5 | 22.7 | 25.1 |
| Senger Creek | 9,700 | 1.7 | 24.4 | 23.4 |
| Blayney Meadows Trail | 7,800 | 3.8 | 28.2 | 19.6 |
| Piute Pass Trail | 8,050 | 1.7 | 29.9 | 17.9 |
| Aspen Meadow | 8,300 | 1.5 | 31.4 | 16.4 |
| South Fork Bridge | 8,350 | 1.3 | 32.7 | 15.1 |
| Goddard Canyon Bridge | 8,450 | 0.8 | 33.5 | 14.3 |
| Evolution Meadow | 9,200 | 2.0 | 35.5 | 12.3 |
| McClure Meadow | 9,600 | 2.0 | 37.5 | 10.3 |
| Colby Meadow | 9,800 | 1.0 | 38.5 | 9.3 |
| Evolution Lake (Lower End) | 10,850 | 3.5 | 42.0 | 5.8 |

| Points on the Route | El. above Sea level | Dist. from pt. above | Dist. from Silver Pass | Dist. to Muir Pass |
|---|---|---|---|---|
| Evolution Lake (Upper End) ....... | 10,850 | 1.3 | 43.3 | 4.5 |
| Muir Pass ...................... | 11,955 | 4.5 | 47.8 | 0.0 |

From *Silver Pass* (10,900—0.0) we descend to

*Silver Pass Lake* (10,350—0.6) to the south. A small rise overlooking the upper end of the lake affords a scenic campsite. (Some timber, rather hard to get at, on cliffs above upper end of lake.) The view across the lake, from the upper end, toward Bear Ridge, Mt. Hilgard and Seven Gables is one of the grandest sights on the Muir Trail between Shadow Lake and Evolution Meadow. The trail skirts the east side of the lake to the lower end and follows above Silver Creek for half a mile and then descends to and crosses to the west bank of the stream which is followed to a large open meadow (several good campsites here, grazing). On the way there is a good view of Mt. Gabb and its glacier, and of a curious broken crater on Bear Ridge called Volcanic Knob. A short distance beyond the meadow we zigzag down a very steep cliff to the upper end of Pocket Meadow in a beautiful box canyon on the

*North Fork of Mono Creek* (8,900—3.0). Here a trail goes upstream to Mott Lake (2 miles) and Bighorn Lake (3.5 miles). Fording the stream, we descend the east bank of the stream for some distance (fine camping and limited grazing in Pocket Meadow; picketing prohibited). Before reaching the main stream of Mono Creek the trail suddenly strikes away from the North Fork. At this point we come to the junction of the

*Mono Pass Trail* (8,300—1.4) (EL 6, see Sec. 3), which branches east from our route, up and around an impassable ridge, and drops down to follow the main stream east to its headwaters, proceeding thence via Mono Pass to Rock Creek Lake (EA 4, see Sec. 2).

The Muir Trail descends to Mono Creek, turns west and crosses the North Fork of Mono Creek. We follow along the north bank on the valley floor to a trail junction one-quarter mile east of Quail Meadow (good camping and stock feed) near

*Mono Creek Bridge* (7,700—1.6). Here the Mono Creek Trail (WL 3, see Sec. 11) continues down Mono Creek past Quail Meadow about a mile and a half to the upper end of Lake Thomas Edison, then follows around the north shore of the lake to the Lake Edison roadhead (6.0) and Vermilion Campground.

At this point our route turns south and crosses the Mono Creek Bridge. We ascend the southeast valley wall up

*Bear Ridge* (9,950—4.6), the divide between Mono Creek and Bear Creek. Views of Vermilion Cliffs across the valley during the ascent. The trail continues across the top of Bear Ridge through forests, passing the junction of an old trail down the ridge to the east end of Vermilion Dam. Later we arrive at the drop-off into Bear Creek, where a fine view of Bear Creek drainage, dominated by Mt. Hilgard and Seven Gables, is enjoyed. The trail descends by steep zigzags to

*Bear Creek* (8,800—2.1) in a wide forested valley, and follows the north bank upstream. Here is met the Bear Creek Trail coming from a road (steep and rough), which branches east from the road to Lake Thomas Edison (see Sec. 8) and terminates at Bear Diversion Dam. Almost immediately after striking the creek we pass into a pleasing meadow at Kip Camp (camping and limited grazing). Continuing along the east bank of Bear Creek, which now comes from the south, and just before arriving at the ford of the Hilgard Branch, we come to the junction of the

*Trail to Lake Italy* (9,250—2.3), which ascends eastward from our route up the Hilgard Branch to its headwaters in that lake. A sign at the junction reads: Lake Italy 7 mi. (See Sec. 5 for description of this trail.) We leave the junction of the Lake Italy Trail and ford the Hilgard Branch (several forks) near its junction with Bear Creek and continue up the east side of Bear Creek. Shortly we pass into a delightful meadow (fine view of Seven Gables, grazing, several rustic campsites on opposite bank of stream), and we come to the junction of the

*Trail to East Fork of Bear Creek Lakes* (9,500—1.2). This trail (rough and hazardous for stock) parallels the east bank of Bear Creek for a short distance, then ascends the East Fork on its north bank (fine camping and limited grazing), later crosses to the south bank and follows the stream to its outlet at about timberline (10,600—3.0) from a small lake at the lower end of a long granite basin containing a string of lovely lakes known as Seven Gables Lakes (10,800) nestling under Seven Gables (13,075). To the east at the headwaters of the forks of the East Fork, lies a high alpine region containing several glacial basins in which are many lakes. The largest are named Vee Lake (11,100), Claw Lake (11,200), Den Lake (11,600), Coronet Lake (11,700), Big Bear Lake (11,400), Ursa Lake (11,400), Bear Paw Lake (11,500), and Black Bear Lake (11,650).

From the trail junction the Muir Trail crosses Bear Creek and, leaving it, ascends the steep wooded canyon of its west fork. At the top of the ascent we pass through some sloping wooded meadows, cross to the east side of Bear Creek, pass a trail junction (trail east to Lou Beverly Lake) and enter a large open meadow which has been named Rosemarie Meadow (fine camping). At the south end of Rosemarie Meadow a trail branches west, fords Bear Creek, and ascends about a mile to Rose Lake, in a beautiful amphitheater under Mt. Hooper (12,349). We continue up the east side of the West Fork of Bear Creek to its headwaters in

*Marie Lake* (10,600—2.6). Our trail skirts the grassy west shore of this double lake and from its upper end we ascend to

*Selden Pass* (10,872—1.3), from which we have an excellent view of the headwaters of Bear Creek dominated by Mt. Hilgard (13,361). We descend from the pass to

*Heart Lake* (10,490—0.7), a small lake shaped like a heart and the uppermost of a chain of four lakes. Below Heart Lake there are beautiful views across the lower lakes to Mts. Henry and Goddard. We descend on the east side of the stream and ford while passing between Sally Keyes Lakes. We cross a large open meadow below and pass the junction of the

*Trail to Blayney Meadows* (10,100—1.3), shown on U.S.G.S. map as following downstream to Blayney Meadows, but very steep and little used. We ford and leave the stream and proceed east from the meadow, crossing several delightful "sky-parlor" meadows (water scarce). We enjoy occasional glimpses of Mt.

Goddard and the vast canyon of the South Fork of San Joaquin River. Finally we ford a fair-sized stream,

*Senger Creek* (9,700—1.7), and arrive in a grassy forested flat (fine camping and grazing). Just beyond it, the trail drops over the rim of the canyon of the South Fork of the San Joaquin, passing the junction of a short-cut trail to Blayney Meadows. Continuing along the trail, we zigzag down to the floor of the valley of the South Fork, and meet the

*Trail to Blayney Meadows and Florence Lake* (7,800—3.8) (WL 4, see Sec. 10), which leads westward down the valley to Blayney Meadows, one of the famous campsites in the Sierra, and thence to Florence Lake at the end of the road from Huntington Lake (WA 2, see Sec. 8).

From the junction we go eastward through a sandy wooded country up the floor of the valley, out of sight of the river, and come to Piute Creek at the junction of the

*Piute Pass Trail* (8,050—1.7) (EL 8, see Sec. 7), which leaves our route and proceeds up Piute Creek via Piute Pass to the road from Bishop at North Lake. We cross Piute Creek near its junction with the South Fork by a bridge located a few yards from the junction of the trails. Here we enter Kings Canyon National Park and continue up the valley, following a rocky gorge along the river. We arrive at

*Aspen Meadow* (8,300—1.5) (camping but no grazing). Continuing south on the trail we soon cross to the southeast bank of the river by the

*South Fork Suspension Bridge* (8,350—1.3). Just beyond the bridge is a stock fence (some ready-made camp spots, but no grazing). Above, Evolution Creek enters the main stream from the east. A short distance above their forks we cross the South Fork, which comes down Goddard Canyon, on the

*Goddard Canyon Bridge* (8,450—0.8). Here is the junction of the Goddard Canyon Trail which ascends the South Fork and leads to the Hell-For-Sure Pass Trail (WL 5, see Sec. 13) passing a trail (not maintained) to Martha Lake (11,000—12.0), the base from which to climb Mt. Goddard. We cross the bridge and go up and around the point dividing the junction of the two streams to the south bank of Evolution Creek, up which we ascend through a steep gorge (grand cascades), fording the creek (high water in early summer) a quarter mile before reaching

*Evolution Meadow* (9,200—2.0). This is the lowest of the three great meadows of Evolution Creek, among the finest in the Sierra. (Fence below Evolution Meadow—excellent camping and grazing.) The higher meadows, McClure and Colby, are a shade greener and fresher than Evolution Meadow. McClure Meadow, the largest and most beautiful of the three, commands a fine view of the Evolution group of peaks. The trail continues along the north side of Evolution Creek for the full length of Evolution Valley.

We now enter the region where the grand crescendo of the Sierra touches at once the heart of the mountaineer and the artist. It is impossible to exaggerate the varied beauty of the scenery along the Muir Trail from Evolution Meadow to Mt. Whitney and the Kern. Leaving Evolution Meadow we soon come to

*McClure Meadow* (9,600—2.0) (closed to grazing until August 1 and possibly later depending upon the condition of the vegetation). Here we find a ranger

station which is manned by a ranger from late June
until early September. We continue up the gently sloping forested floor of Evolution Valley to

*Colby Meadow* (9,800—1.0) (good camping but
closed to grazing until August 1 and possibly later depending upon the condition of the vegetation), dominated by The Hermit and the cliffs of the Evolution
group of peaks. We continue up the valley, passing a
small meadow south of the trail at its upper end (good
camping here is often overlooked; grazing and grand
cascades) and then ascend a steep cliff. Passing the
eastern lateral over Lamarck Col which takes off the
end of a switchback a mile below Evolution Lake (see
Sec. 7), we come to the

*Lower End of Evolution Lake* (10,850—3.5). (No
wood fires permitted from here to Muir Pass; no grazing for pack and saddle stock; burros and walking
mules one night only.) This beautiful lake has long
grassy shores and is surrounded by high, desolate
granite cliffs and peaks. It is one of the most impressive lakes in the Sierra. There is a grand view across it
from the lower end to the pyramid-shaped Mts. Hux-
ley and Spencer. As one approaches the upper end,
the Goddard Divide with its extensive snowfields
comes into view. The lower end of Evolution Lake is
the last sheltered campsite for 9 miles, for there is a
total absence of timber beyond until one reaches the
small lakes below Helen Lake on the other side of
Muir Pass; many go on to Little Pete Meadow. Camp-
ers should limit their stay at Evolution Lake due to its
fragile nature. The vicinity of Evolution Lake is a
mecca for mountain climbers because of the proximity
of The Hermit and Mts. Fiske, Wallace, Haeckel, and

Darwin. The trail skirts the east shore of the lake to the

*Upper End of Evolution Lake* (10,850—1.3). Above, we cross the inlet stream and continue up a rocky canyon, later skirting the grassy wet shore of the long narrow Sapphire Lake (grand view of Mt. Darwin) and an irregular-shaped lake above, then fording the stream and striking the lower end of Wanda Lake (11,452), from which a closer view is enjoyed of Mt. Goddard and the extensive snowfields on the Goddard Divide. Wanda Lake is the starting point of the approach to Mt. Goddard from this side.

The Muir Trail goes up the east side of the lake, and approximately midway leaves the lake, passing a small lake above, and ascends a fairly steep rocky slope to

*Muir Pass* (11,955—4.5). From this pass (named for John Muir, whose name and work this Guide is intended to perpetuate) one enjoys a strange view back at Wanda Lake and its barren surroundings and of the forbidding crags and summits on either side of the pass. Here the Sierra Club erected a stone shelter with the aid of the Forest Service through the generosity of the late George Frederick Schwarz, dedicated to the memory of John Muir, and designed to provide shelter from storm upon this high and exposed pass. It is intended for public use; but let me remind you to be considerate of the needs of others who may follow. No wood fires are permitted, and due to human sanitation problems it is urged that the hut be used only for emergency overnight stays.

Muir Pass is the key to the rugged barrier, Goddard Divide, which made a trail route difficult from the headwaters of the San Joaquin to the Middle Fork of

Kings River. Before the Muir Trail was made it was necessary to make a long detour via Hell-For-Sure Pass and the North Fork of the Kings to reach the Middle Fork at Simpson Meadow.

### Sec. 2. Eastern Approach No. 4

*Rock Creek Lake
(Inyo National Forest;
Head of Rock Creek–Mono Pass Region)*

*Reached by auto:* On road leaving Highway 395 at Tom's Place, 22 miles north of Bishop—nine miles of paved road to Rock Creek Pack Station, one mile dirt beyond.

*Reached by bus:* Daily, between Los Angeles and Reno to Tom's Place.

*Accommodations:* Lodge below Rock Creek Lake, Tom's Place.

*Supplies:* Rock Creek Lake Store, Rock Creek Lodge, Tom's Place.

*Pack stock, guides:* Station above Rock Creek Lake Store.

This long chain of lakes, with unusually impressive high mountain surroundings, is one of the best scenic playgrounds and fishing resorts of the Owens Valley region.

From its headwaters Rock Creek runs northward down Little Lakes Valley for a distance of about 6 miles, paralleling the main crest. The valley is a high glacial basin heading in the glaciers under Mts. Abbot and Dade. It contains a large number of lakes, and is made accessible by a road which goes part way up

Little Lakes Valley from which a trail leads to the upper end of the basin and then goes over Morgan Pass (10,800), to the Morgan Lakes.

## Sec. 3. Eastern Lateral No. 6

### *Mono Pass Trail*

| Rock Creek Lakes to Mono Creek | El. above Sea level | Dist. from pt. above | Total distance | |
|---|---|---|---|---|
| Road in Little Lakes Valley ........ | 10,300 | 0.0 | 0.0 | 15.0 |
| Mono Pass ...................... | 12,000 | 3.0 | 3.0 | 12.0 |
| Second Recess on Mono Creek ..... | 8,500 | 8.0 | 11.0 | 4.0 |
| Muir Trail at Mono Creek .......... | 8,300 | 4.0 | 15.0 | 0.0 |

Starting from the road in Little Lakes Valley the Mono Pass Trail climbs out on the west side and ascends to the crest of the Sierra at

*Mono Pass* (12,000—3.0). From the summit of Mt. Starr (12,870) (named for the author) just north of the pass, there is a wonderfully fine view looking southward toward Mt. Humphreys, Bear Creek Spire, Mt. Dade and Mt. Abbot, and northward over the Pioneer Basin, surrounded by Mts. Huntington, Stanford, Crocker and Hopkins to Red-and-White Mountain. Scores of lakes can be counted. From the pass the trail drops down into the headwaters of Mono Creek, with its charming recesses.

From the upper forks, knapsackers may explore the Fourth Recess and its lakes. Northward, animals can be taken into Pioneer Basin with its many beautiful lakes (camping and grazing).

Another trail leaves the Mono Pass Trail half a mile above its crossing of Hopkins Creek, ascends to and crosses to the west side of the stream and zigzags steeply up to Lower Hopkins Lake (10,600), where lovely campsites will be found.

A rough trail leads up Third Recess to Third Recess Lake (10,500), (camping and grazing). Fish Camp, a good campsite, is opposite the

*Second Recess* (8,500—8.0), which also has a rough trail part way up. Our trail follows down the deep, beautiful canyon of Mono Creek on the north side to the

*Muir Trail* (8,300—4.0) at the North Fork of Mono Creek above its junction with the main stream.

### Sec. 4. Eastern Approach No. 5

#### *Round Valley*

The Owens River, flowing down from Long Valley, enters Round Valley—a level valley floor bounded by the Sierra on the west and the Volcanic Tableland on the east. Here Rock Creek (entering the valley at its northern end), Pine Creek (from the west), and Horton Creek (from the south) join the Owens River, which flows out of the southeastern end of Round Valley, between the Tungsten Hills and Volcanic Tableland, into the long reaches of Owens Valley.

From Round Valley, a few miles north of Bishop on Highway 395, a road goes up the great canyon of Pine Creek ten miles to the forks near its headwaters. Here pack and saddle stock are available. A trail (EL 7) continues up the main stream and over Pine Creek Pass to meet the Piute Pass Trail (EL 8) at Hutchinson Meadow on Piute Creek.

From EL 7 a trail branches west at the head of Pine Creek, ascends to the crest through Granite Park and after crossing Italy Pass (see Sec. 5) south of Mt. Julius Caesar (13,196) descends via Lake Italy to the Muir Trail at Bear Creek. This scenic trail may be difficult to follow at times and is not passable to livestock on the west side of the crest.

### Sec. 5. Eastern Lateral No. 7

#### *Pine Creek Pass Trail*

| Pine Creek to Hutchinson Meadow and Muir Trail at S.F. San Joaquin River via EL 7 (see Sec. 9) | El. above Sea level | Dist. from pt. above | Total distance | |
|---|---|---|---|---|
| Pine Creek Road ................ | 7,400 | 0.0 | 0.0 | 20.0 |
| Pine Lake ...................... | 9,950 | 3.5 | 3.5 | 16.5 |
| Junction Lateral to Lake Italy ...... | 10,200 | 1.5 | 5.0 | 15.0 |
| Pine Creek Pass .................. | 11,100 | 2.0 | 7.0 | 13.0 |
| Piute Pass Trail EL 8 (Hutchinson Meadow) ...................... | 9,450 | 7.0 | 14.0 | 6.0 |
| Muir Trail S.F. San Joaquin River ... | 8,000 | 6.0 | 20.0 | 0.0 |

From the road in the great canyon of Pine Creek near its forks (7,400), the Pine Creek Pass Trail makes a long, steep climb up the south side of the main stream, fording to the north bank below

*Pine Lake* (9,950—3.5) (camping and grazing), and passes around the north lakeshore. From Pine Lake the trail follows up the east side of the main inlet stream, passes a small lake, fords the inlet and, a short distance above, passes a branching

*Trail to Lake Italy* (10,200—1.5) (see below). Ascending southward up a sloping basin, we cross the Sierra Crest at

*Pine Creek Pass* (11,100—2.0) and descend into a basin at the headwaters of the north fork of Piute Creek, containing many lakes. Our trail follows the stream down French Canyon to

*Hutchinson Meadow* (9,450—7.0) at the forks of Piute Creek (fair camping and grazing). (About 2 miles before reaching Hutchinson Meadow there is a meadow with camping and fine grazing.) Here we meet the Piute Pass Trail EL 8 (see Sec. 7) which we may follow down the west side of Piute Creek to its junction with the South Fork of San Joaquin River where is met the

*Muir Trail* (8,000—6.0).

### Lake Italy Trail (38)
### From EL 7 at Pine Creek
### to Muir Trail at Bear Creek

| Pine Creek to Bear Creek | El. above Sea level | Dist. from pt. above | Total distance | |
|---|---|---|---|---|
| Pine Creek Road ................. | 7,400 | 0.0 | 0.0 | 18.0 |
| Trail Junction above Pine Lake ..... | 10,200 | 5.0 | 5.0 | 13.0 |
| Italy Pass........................ | 12,350 | 4.0 | 9.0 | 9.0 |
| Jumble Lake ..................... | 11,500 | 1.0 | 10.0 | 8.0 |
| Lake Italy ....................... | 11,154 | 0.5 | 10.5 | 7.5 |
| Lake Italy (west end) .............. | 11,154 | 1.0 | 11.5 | 6.5 |
| Muir Trail at Bear Creek .......... | 9,300 | 6.5 | 18.0 | 0.0 |

From the road EL 7 is followed up Pine Creek past Pine Lake to a ford at the inlet to the small lake above. Beyond the ford this trail branches west from EL 7 at the

*Trail Junction* (10,200—5.0) and, crossing the stream, ascends to the glaciated lake basin of Granite Park. Following up a low divide between the two chains of lakes from the head of the basin brings you to

*Italy Pass* (12,350—4.0) (impassable to livestock) over the Sierra Crest just south of Mt. Julius Caesar (13,196) with fine views southeastward down the Sierra Crest to Humphreys Basin and westward into the Lake Italy Basin surrounded by Mts. Hilgard

(13,361), Gabb (13,711), Abbot (13,715), Dade (13,635) and Bear Creek Spire (13,713). From the pass our trail descends to the northwest end of

*Jumble Lake* (11,500—1.0) immediately below to the west, crosses its outlet downstream 0.3 mile to the west side and descends to the southern shore of

*Lake Italy* (11,154—0.5). Turning westward we follow above its southern shores to the

*West end of Lake Italy* (11,154—1.0). Turning southward down the outlet stream (Hilgard Branch of Bear Creek) we cross the small outlet coming from Brown Bear and Teddy Bear lakes, nearby to the east, and about 1 mile below the outlet of Lake Italy descend to and ford the stream to the north side in an open box canyon with grassy, sparsely timbered floor. At the upper end is a ready-made camp. This is the first camping spot with wood, water, and feed since leaving Pine Creek. Elevations above 11,000 feet in this region are above timberline. Our trail leads down the canyon for a mile. Here the floor drops, the canyon bends to the northwest and the stream cascades and drops into the lower valley. The trail zigzags down to the valley below. This lower valley has many delightful meadows (camping and grazing). At the lower end of the valley the canyon makes another turn to the southwest and the trail soon crosses the stream coming from Hilgard Lake. The valley opens up and we proceed along a large open meadow (camping and grazing), following the north side of the stream until the trail descends a low cliff to Bear Creek and meets the

*Muir Trail* (9,300—6.5).

## Sec. 6. Eastern Approach No. 6

*North Fork of Bishop Creek*
*(Inyo National Forest;*
*Lake Sabrina–Piute Pass Region)*

*Reached by auto:* Over road from Highway 395 at Bishop. The road crosses the valley floor to the west and ascends the north bank of Bishop Creek. Wilderness permits at entry station halfway up the creek. Above this the road forks. Take the road up the South Fork for Parchers Camp and South Lake and the road up North Fork for Lake Sabrina and North Lake.

*Reached by bus:* Daily, Los Angeles and Reno to Bishop. Arrangements can be made at Bishop for taxi to roadheads.

*Airplane:* Scheduled flights daily from Los Angeles.

*Information and Wilderness Permits:* Entrance station halfway up Bishop Creek or Forest Service office in Bishop.

*Accommodations:* Cardinal Lodge. Campgrounds above and below lodge.

*Supplies:* Store at Cardinal Lodge and Bishop.

*Saddle and pack stock, guides:* Station at North Lake.

One and a half miles up the valley above Cardinal Lodge is *Lake Sabrina,* from the upper end of which a mountain trail of several miles brings one to Blue Lake, a beautiful spot. The head of the basin in which this lake lies is under the east side of the Evolution group of peaks (Darwin, Wallace, Haeckel, and Powell).

Below Lake Sabrina a road branches to *North Lake* on the North Fork of Bishop Creek.

## Sec. 7. Eastern Lateral No. 8

### *Piute Pass Trail*

| North Lake to S.F. San Joaquin | El. above Sea level | Dist. from pt. above | Total distance | |
|---|---|---|---|---|
| North Lake | 9,200 | 0.0 | 0.0 | 18.0 |
| Piute Pass | 11,400 | 6.0 | 6.0 | 12.0 |
| Golden Trout Lake | 10,800 | 2.0 | 8.0 | 10.0 |
| Hutchinson Meadow (Junction EL 7) | 9,450 | 4.0 | 12.0 | 6.0 |
| Muir Trail at South Fork of San Joaquin | 8,050 | 6.0 | 18.0 | 0.0 |

Follow the road past

*North Lake* (9,200—0.0) where a fine view of the Evolution group of peaks is enjoyed, to the road end west of the lake. No overnight backpacker parking beyond the upper end of the lake. Here we come to the Piute Pass Trail. Starting up the trail we pass through pretty, flowery, wooded and meadowed country for some distance. (Good camping and grazing.) We then ascend through forested country, finding several small meadows (camping and grazing), to a chain of high lakes (sparse timber and meadows suitable for camping almost to top of pass) above which we reach the summit at

*Piute Pass* (11,400—6.0). Beyond lies Humphreys Basin, open and desolate-appearing, surrounded by the forbidding cliffs of Mt. Humphreys and the Glacier Divide. The floor of the basin is strewn with numerous lakes. We descend from the pass into the basin which forms the headwaters of Piute Creek, passing several small lakes. The timber is sparse until we arrive at the lowest lake in the basin.

*Golden Trout Lake* (10,800—2.0). (Camping and grazing—imposing view of Mt. Humphreys.) It is an easy day's trip from North Lake over the pass to this point. Beyond Golden Trout Lake the trail drops down a steep canyon from the lower southwest end of Humphreys Basin, descending to

*Hutchinson Meadow* (9,450—4.0), at the junction of Piute Creek with its north fork in French Canyon. Hutchinson Meadow, although scenically not as grand as Humphreys Basin above, offers the best camping and grazing on the Piute Pass Trail. Here we meet EL 7 (see Sec. 5).

There are good camping and grazing spots for some distance down Piute Creek, then a long distance with no grazing—Evolution Meadow and Senger Creek on the Muir Trail and Blayney Meadows on the lateral to Florence Lake being the nearest. From the lower end of Hutchinson Meadow valley our route descends a narrow steep gorge, scaling above and descending again to the stream several times until we arrive upon the floor of the long valley of the South Fork of San Joaquin River, where we strike the

*Muir Trail* (8,050—6.0) at the bridge across Piute Creek.

### *Lamarck Col-North Lake*
### *to the Muir Trail at Evolution Lake*

Lamarck Col has now evolved from a cross-country route into a marginal trail. Although it is the shortest route into the Evolution country, still at 12,900 feet it is one of the highest and most rugged passes in the Sierra that barely has a trail over it. From the end of the road at North Lake take the Lamarck Lakes trail past Grass Lake. Passing the east end of Lower Lamarck Lake, the trail turns south to switchback along the side of a steep spur and fades out going west again over a series of sand flats toward the last steep snowfield up to the col. On the west side drop southward over talus toward the highest of the Darwin Lakes, where it becomes a trail again, going along the north side of the lakes to Darwin Bench. Here we switch to the south side of the creek and drop steeply down to intersect the Muir Trail a mile below Evolution Lake. Darwin Bench has been overcamped; camping is better below there toward the Muir Trail.

### Sec. 8. Western Approach No. 2

*Huntington Lake, Florence Lake
and Lake Thomas Edison
(Sierra National Forest;
South Fork of San Joaquin River Region)*

*Reached by auto:* From Fresno. Distance to Huntington Lake, 64 miles. Distance from Huntington Lake (upper end) to Florence Lake, 22 miles via oiled mountain road.

*Accommodations:* Huntington Lake resorts; meals and lodging available at Mono Hot Springs. A well-developed campground with facilities for hot mineral baths is maintained by the Forest Service and the concessionaire at Mono Hot Springs.

*Supplies:* Huntington Lake, Mono Hot Springs, and Florence Lake.

*Pack and saddle stock, guides:* Huntington Lake, Mono Hot Springs, and Florence Lake. Boat for hire at Florence Lake for transportation to upper end of lake.

Huntington Lake is a reservoir on the site of the

former Home Camp Meadow. Notwithstanding its artificial character, it is a popular resort.

Florence Lake is a natural lake which has been enlarged by a dam. Lake Thomas Edison was created by a dam on Mono Creek which floods Vermilion Valley. These reservoirs are part of the hydroelectric system of the Southern California Edison Company. The road from Huntington Lake leads to both dams. Forking about a mile east of the High Sierra Ranger Station, the north-branching road goes to Mono Hot Springs and Vermilion Campground at the west end of Lake Edison. Ahead, the road leads to Florence Lake. Here starts the Blayney Meadows Trail (WL 4, see Sec. 10) leading to the Muir Trail.

### Sec. 9. Western Laterals No. 3

*From the Lake Edison Road*
*to the Muir Trail on Mono Creek*
*and Bear Creek; Goodale Pass Trail*

About a mile north of Mono Hot Springs on the road to Lake Edison, a steep and rough road branches east to Bear Creek (7,350—2.0). From its end the Bear Creek Trail follows up Bear Creek to meet the Muir Trail (8,800—6.5) after its descent from Bear Ridge (see p. 104).

From the end of the road at Vermilion Campground at the west end of Lake Edison, a trail follows above the northern shore of the lake and then follows up Mono Creek a mile and a half through Quail Meadow to a junction with the Muir Trail at the bridge across Mono Creek (see p. 104). (From here the Mono Pass Trail, (see Sec. 3) and the Muir Trail are the same for a mile and a half.)

From the north shore of Lake Edison the Goodale Pass Trail branches north to cross the Silver Divide at Goodale Pass (11,000), meeting the Muir Trail at the head of a tributary of Fish Creek (see Part 1, p. 86).

### Sec. 10. Western Lateral No. 4

*Blayney Meadows Trail From Florence Lake to the Muir Trail above Blayney Meadows*

Leaving the end of the road at Florence Lake the Blayney Meadows Trail skirts the lake on the west side and follows up the South Fork of San Joaquin River, traversing Blayney Meadows, and eventually meeting the Muir Trail (9.0). Good hot springs at Blayney Meadows Campground.

### Sec. 11. Huntington Lake-Silver Creek Trail (36-37)

*From Huntington Lake to Fish Creek Valley*

Leaving the road near Deer Creek at the upper end of
   *Huntington Lake* (7,000—0.0), this trail ascends northeastward over Kaiser Ridge at
   *Potter Pass* (9,000—4.2). From Kaiser Peak (10,320) nearby there is a sweeping view across the basin of the San Joaquin to the Sierra Crest from Ritter and The Minarets nearly to Humphreys. The trail descends below Twin Lakes to cross
   *Sample Meadows* (8,000—4.0). After rounding a point on a low ridge the trail descends on the northern side of Rattlesnake Creek to the
   *South Fork of San Joaquin River* (6,000—5.0) which is crossed on a steel suspension bridge. After climbing out of the canyon the trail goes northward above its eastern rim and then follows up Rock Creek to

*Rock Creek Crossing* (7,000—7.0). A mile short of the crossing the San Joaquin River Trail (36) from Mono Creek meets our trail. From the crossing this trail goes on to Granite Creek Campground (see Part II, Sec. 12) while our trail follows up Rock Creek to its headwaters near

*Rock Creek Lake* (9,200—5.0). Here a trail branches to Margaret Lakes (10,000—5.0), a beautiful lake basin west of the Silver Divide where peaks rise to almost 12,000 feet. Our trail descends northward to

*String Meadows* (8,500—3.0) where it turns eastward to cross

*Silver Creek* (8,000—2.0). Near the crossing another trail to Margaret Lakes continues up the stream about 5 miles.

From the crossing of Silver Creek the trail descends down the canyon wall and meets the Crater Creek-Fish Creek Trail (AR 5, see Part II, Sec. 2) in

*Fish Valley* (6,400—3.5). The distance from Huntington Lake to Fish Valley is about 34 miles.

## Sec. 12. Western Approach No. 3

*North Fork of Kings River*
*(Sierra National Forest)*

*Reached by auto:* From Fresno or Madera by the road branching east from the Huntington Lake Road south of Shaver Lake.

*Accommodations and Supplies:* Dinkey Creek and Wishon Dam.

*Saddle, pack stock, guides:* Dinkey Creek, Wishon Dam, and Courtright Reservoir.

The North Fork of Kings River is a much smaller

stream than the South and Middle forks, having a watershed which does not reach back to the Sierra Crest. Its headwaters are confined by the Le Conte Divide, a secondary crest separating them from the Middle Fork. On the western slope of the divide the North Fork gathers its waters and flows southwestward into the main Kings River.

While not so rugged as the mountain area along the main crest of the Sierra, this region has great attraction, abounding in beautiful forests, meadows, and lakes, with peaks along the crest of the Le Conte Divide rising to about 12,000 feet. Here the rolling country and lower elevations combine with a lack of crowding to make this fine backpacking country, especially for beginners.

The Pacific Gas and Electric company has made two reservoirs in this area. A dam on the North Fork of Kings River floods Coolidge Meadow to make Wishon Reservoir. One on the Helms Creek Fork floods Sand Meadows to make Courtright Reservoir. From Dinkey Creek and the two dams a system of trails traverse this region. The abundance of fine campsites and feed for stock makes it attractive for travel.

### Sec. 13. Western Laterals No. 5

*Western Lateral No. 5A –*
*Hell-For-Sure Pass Trail*

| *Courtright Dam to Goddard Canyon* | El. above Sea level | Dist. from pt. above | Total distance | |
|---|---|---|---|---|
| Courtright Dam .................. | 8,150 | 0.0 | 0.0 | 25.5 |
| Maxson Meadows ............... | 8,150 | 2.5 | 2.5 | 23.0 |
| Florence Lake Trail .............. | 8,900 | 2.0 | 4.5 | 21.0 |

| Courtright Dam to Goddard Canyon | El. above Sea level | Dist. from pt. above | Total distance | |
|---|---|---|---|---|
| Blackcap Basin Trail .............. | 8,200 | 3.5 | 8.0 | 17.5 |
| Trail from Wishon Dam (WL 5B).... | 10,200 | 7.0 | 15.0 | 10.5 |
| Hell-For-Sure Pass ............... | 11,300 | 2.5 | 17.5 | 8.0 |
| South Fork San Joaquin River ...... | 9,500 | 3.0 | 20.5 | 5.0 |
| Muir Trail-Goddard Canyon Bridge . | 8,450 | 5.0 | 25.5 | 0.0 |

From *Courtright Dam* (8,150) this trail goes north on the east side of the reservoir to

*Maxson Meadows* (8,150—2.5) where it forks. Our trail turns east of Maxson Dome where the

*Florence Lake Trail* (8,900—2.0) (see Sec. 10) branches north, by which it is 11 miles to the Blayney Meadows Trail. At Long Meadow (1.5) another trail branches north to join it. Turning east and then south along Post Corral Creek we come to the junction of the

*Blackcap Basin Trail* (8,200—3.5) leading to Blackcap Basin, described in WL No. 5B (see page 126). Our trail turns eastward over a divide, then northward past Fleming Lake, where we turn eastward to the junction with

*WL No. 5B* (10,200—7.0). Proceeding eastward north of Disappointment Lake and Hell-For-Sure Lake we climb steeply over

*Hell-For-Sure Pass* (11,300—2.5) at the top of the Le Conte Divide and enter Kings Canyon National Park. From the pass the trail zigzags down under Red Mountain (11,951) and then turns southward up Goddard Canyon, descending the west wall to the

*South Fork of San Joaquin River* (9,900—3.0). Upstream a route (trail not maintained) goes 4 miles to the headwaters at Martha Lake (11,000). Our trail follows the canyon downstream to the junction of the

*Muir Trail* (8,450—5.0) at the Goddard Canyon

Bridge, just above the forks of Evolution Creek and the main stream. (Good camping and grazing 1 mile above junction.)

### *Western Lateral No. 5B*
### *to Hell-For-Sure Pass Trail*

| *Wishon Dam to WL No. 5A* | El. above Sea level | Dist. from pt. above | Total distance | |
|---|---|---|---|---|
| Wishon Dam . . . . . . . . . . . . . . . . . . . . . | 6,500 | 0.0 | 0.0 | 21.5 |
| Crown Valley Trail . . . . . . . . . . . . . . . | 8,400 | 5.0 | 5.0 | 16.5 |
| Head of Nichols Canyon Trail Junction . . . . . . . . . . . . . . . . . . | 10,188 | 5.5 | 10.5 | 11.0 |
| North Fork Kings River Blackcap Basin Trail . . . . . . . . . . . | 8,400 | 2.4 | 12.9 | 8.6 |
| Hell-For-Sure Pass Trail . . . . . . . . . . | 10,200 | 8.6 | 21.5 | 0.0 |

From the east end of *Wishon Dam* (6,500) a trail leads northward to meet the old Woodchuck Trail leading eastward. After passing the junction of the south-branching

*Crown Valley Trail* (8,400—5.0) our trail trends northeastward to the junction of a branching trail to Woodchuck Lake and then eastward to

*The Head of Nichols Canyon* (10,188—5.5). Here two trails branch. One goes south to Crown Valley (8.5) and one goes via Halfmoon Lake to Blackcap Basin (8.0). From the northeastern rim of this basin a knapsack route goes over the Le Conte Divide to Martha Lake, headwaters of the South Fork of the San Joaquin River, lying below Mt. Goddard (13,568). From the lake Goddard may be easily climbed.

The trail down Nichols Canyon is no longer maintained, and our best route is to descend to Halfmoon Lake and follow the outlet stream to the

*Blackcap Basin Trail* (8,400—2.4) on the North

Fork of the Kings River. This trail leads upstream to the basin described above (8.4).

Heading downstream we pass the Fall Creek Trail (not maintained) branching eastward to a series of glacial basins, extending to the Le Conte Divide, containing many beautiful lakes.

Soon we come to the junction of a trail leading north. Here we leave the Blackcap Basin Trail, which downstream goes northwest to meet the Hell-For-Sure Pass Trail on Post Corral Creek (5.0), and follow the north-branching trail, past Devils Punchbowl, to

*Hell-For-Sure Pass Trail* (10,200—7.0), near Disappointment Lake. This route is about 5 miles longer than WL No. 5A to this point, but it traverses a much more interesting region.

### *Crown Valley-Tehipite Trail*

About three miles south of Wishon Dam (6,600) a trail leaves the road to the east and crosses a pass (8,600) leading to Crown Valley (8,400—12.0). Here is the junction of several trails including the Tehipite-Middle Fork Trail (see Part IV, Secs. 6 and 7). The Jeep trail from Wishon now goes almost to Crown Valley.

# PART IV:
# Middle Fork of Kings River Region

This part of the Muir Trail is one of its most attractive sections, with its contrasts of beautiful streams, meadows and canyons, and high mountain basins in their background of rugged peaks. The trail descends from Muir Pass down the Middle Fork of Kings River from its headwaters in Helen Lake to Little Pete Meadow, and then follows the floor of the tremendous Le Conte Canyon to Grouse Meadow.

Between Grouse Meadow and the South Fork of Kings River there was long a gap in the construction of the John Muir Trail. Two routes were proposed, one up Palisade Creek and across Mather Pass, the other by way of Cartridge Creek. The former was originally selected as part of the official trail by J. N. LeConte, of the Sierra Club, who pioneered the trail routes and peaks of the High Sierra for many years and who has contributed so much of the lore of these mountains to others in issues of the *Sierra Club Bulletin*. The Mather Pass route is through a higher and more rugged region and to me has more scenic attraction. The trail up Palisade Creek follows close to this beautiful stream in a narrow, deep valley. At the head of the valley is Deer Meadow. From here the north wall of the valley rises to the Sierra Crest, dominated by North Palisade. The south wall rises to the crest of a high divide, separating the watersheds of Palisade Creek and Cartridge Creek. From one of its summits, Observation Peak, there are wonderful views of the Palisades and of the nearby high glacier basin, with its lakes, at the head of Cataract Creek, which hurtles down to join Palisade Creek in Deer Meadow.

## Sec. 1. The John Muir Trail

### *Muir Pass to Mather Pass*

| Points on the Route | El. above Sea level | Dist. from pt. above | Dist. from Muir Pass | Dist. to Mather Ps. |
|---|---|---|---|---|
| Muir Pass ........................ | 11,955 | 0.0 | 0.0 | 22.0 |
| Helen Lake ........................ | 11,595 | 1.0 | 1.0 | 21.0 |
| Le Conte Canyon-Upper Lake Camp | 10,800 | 1.3 | 2.3 | 19.7 |
| Le Conte Canyon-Lower Lake Camp | 10,200 | 1.0 | 3.3 | 18.7 |
| Little Pete Meadow ............... | 8,800 | 3.5 | 6.8 | 15.2 |
| Bishop Pass Trail ................. | 8,700 | 0.5 | 7.3 | 14.7 |
| Grouse Meadows ................. | 8,200 | 3.2 | 10.5 | 11.5 |

| Points on the Route | El. above Sea level | Dist. from pt. above | Dist. from Muir Pass | Dist. to Mather Ps. |
|---|---|---|---|---|
| Middle Fork Trail ................ | 8,000 | 1.0 | 11.5 | 10.5 |
| Deer Meadow (lower end) ........ | 8,700 | 3.5 | 15.0 | 7.0 |
| Palisade Lake (lower) ............ | 10,650 | 3.0 | 18.0 | 4.0 |
| Mather Pass ..................... | 12,080 | 4.0 | 22.0 | 0.0 |

From

*Muir Pass* (11,955—0.0) we descend a steep talus slope to Helen Lake. This large desolate lake is situated in a high rocky basin surrounded by rugged peaks and precipices. The trail skirts the southeast shore to the

*East Side of Helen Lake* (11,595—1.0), whence we descend a steep cliff into a narrow rocky gorge, keeping close to the stream. Beyond, we descend a difficult cliff to a small rock-bound lake (fine view down Le Conte Canyon). Soon we arrive at a larger lake with grassy shores (scant timber), the first campsite below Muir Pass, which may be called

*Le Conte Canyon-Upper Lake Camp* (10,800—1.3). We turn southward down a sparsely timbered valley, fording the stream to the west bank and later returning to the east bank, passing several small lakes at some distance from the trail. We ford a small tributary stream and arrive at

*Le Conte Canyon-Lower Lake Camp* (10,200—1.0), on the border of a delightful grassy basin in which a small lake reposes a short distance south of the trail, with imposing cliffs rising beyond it. This lake is the lowest lake we pass on the Middle Fork of Kings River.

At the lakelet the valley makes an abrupt turn eastward and the stream hurtles into it by a fall over a cliff below the lake. We descend a steep cliff where the trail is cut in a perpendicular granite wall, and zigzag down toward the stream (view of the falls). We proceed down the north bank of the stream in an easterly direction through a steep rocky gorge. Gradually the valley floor flattens out, curves southward and becomes more wooded. Later, in a thickly forested flat (a favorite campsite of mine, more secluded), we pass a small open meadow south of the trail, and half a mile farther on arrive at

*Little Pete Meadow* (8,800—3.5). This long open meadow, flanked on either side by high Yosemite-like cliffs, and Grouse Meadows, some distance below it, afford the most popular camping and grazing grounds on the Middle Fork of Kings River. However, overgrazing in past years has greatly limited available forage, so pack outfits should restrict their stay here. The trail follows close to the east bank of this beautiful stream all the way from Little Pete Meadow to the junction of Palisade Creek below Grouse Meadows. From the lower end of Little Pete Meadow we descend a short steep gorge, beyond which the valley floor flattens out again for some distance. Near the junction of Dusy Creek, which plunges down a steep granite slope from the east, we reach the junction of the

*Bishop Pass Trail* (EL 9, see Sec. 3) (8,700—0.5). The Le Conte Canyon Ranger Station is located just north of the Bishop Pass Trail Junction. The signs at the junction read: *(north)* Muir Pass 8 mi., McClure Meadow 18 mi., *(south)* Grouse Meadows 3 mi., *(east)* Dusy Basin 4 mi., Bishop Pass 7 mi., South Lake 14 mi.

Our route continues down the east bank of the deep forested canyon of the Middle Fork, with high glaciated cliffs and basins above (their size is best appreciated from the extreme lower end of Dusy Basin on the Bishop Pass Trail) to

*Grouse Meadows* (8,200—3.2). This refreshing open meadow is one of the most delightful spots in the High Sierra. Due to boggy sod it is difficult to find a campsite conveniently close to the stream. My choice is the spot at the extreme upper end of the meadow on the river side of the trail, close to a tiny tributary stream. We leave the meadow and continue down the canyon of the Middle Fork to the mouth of Palisade Creek where we meet the

*Middle Fork Trail* (WL 6, see Sec. 6) (8,000—1.0) coming up the canyon. From the junction our trail leaves the Middle Fork and turns up the north bank of Palisade Creek. In about a mile we arrive at an aspen flat where there is a good ready-made campsite and a fine view downstream toward the black pinnacles of the Devil's Crags. The trail continues along the north bank, through forests and meadows (good camp, grazing) to the

*Lower End of Deer Meadow* (8,700—3.5). This is a long meadow (fine camping and grazing), the floor of which is partly covered with thick timber and underbrush. Deer Meadow lies at the head of a deep valley. At the upper end the valley floor terminates abruptly at the mouth of a precipitous and rocky gorge leading to the headwaters of Palisade Creek. Two tributary streams hurtle into Deer Meadow down the steep north valley wall.

At the extreme upper end of the meadow we emerge at the mouth of the precipitous rocky gorge at the head of the valley. Steeply the trail ascends the gorge over talus on the north bank of Palisade Creek. Some distance up the gorge at the base of a steep impassable cliff (falls) the route mounts several ledges to the north and away from the stream (the Golden Stairway). Above the cliff the route turns back toward the stream and descends by a short steep ledge to its bank in a narrow rocky channel. The mighty pinnacles of Middle Palisade now come into view above a ridge in the foreground. This is one of the most impressive mountain masses in the range. We soon arrive at the lower end of a beautiful lake which I shall call

*Lower Palisade Lake* (10,650—3.0). From here the crest of the Palisades dominates the scene. Many who have looked down from the peaks on the Sierra Crest will agree that the view from the Palisade group is the grandest. The elevation is over 14,000 feet, but, more important, the view south over the great culmination of the Sierra Crest looks toward the northern slopes of the peaks and spurs where lie the snowfields and many of the ancient glacial amphitheaters. The Sierra, like other ranges, is far more beautiful and impressive when dressed with snowfields and glaciers, to contrast with massive rock and nestling lakes. Below the eastern sheer wall of the Palisades lie their own glaciers. To the west is the high Goddard Divide and the rugged spurs between. To the south, extending to the Kaweah Peaks, the view is indescribable. Mt. Sill has the advantage in position over other Palisade summits, and it can therefore be said to be the peer of all Sierra peaks in the extent and quality of its views. It can be climbed without danger or difficulty (though it is a strenuous all-day project) if the following route is taken:

From the outlet of Lower Palisade Lake, go north over a rocky divide and contour into the headwaters of Glacier Creek above a large lake. Continue up the creek to its head in a small sloping glacier where the canyon ends against the crest. From the foot of this glacier the summit of Mt. Sill is not seen. The summits to the west, beyond the upper end of the glacier, are on the crest extending from North Palisade, almost as high, but separated from the highest spire by a deep chasm. To climb Mt. Sill you boldy and blindly take the steep, rocky wall on the right (east) side of the amphitheater, starting from the right lower end of the glacier, and ascend away from it. Twenty or thirty minutes of climbing takes you to the top.

Going around the north side of Lower Palisade Lake along open grassy benches on the cliffs above the shoreline, we ascend to the even more beautiful upper lake. Its shore is grassy and sparsely timbered and affords the highest camping and grazing on the headwaters of Palisade Creek. We traverse above and east of this lake, ford a tributary stream, and continue up rocky benches to the head of the basin. A low gap on the crest immediately south leads to the headwaters of the South Fork of Kings River, and we zigzag through the rough talus to the gap, which is

*Mather Pass* (12,080—4.0). A superb view is enjoyed from the pass northward to the Palisades and southeastward to the Upper Basin of the South Fork of Kings River dominated by Split Mountain (originally South Palisade). This is the southernmost of the Palisade group of 14,000-foot peaks, and can be easily climbed from the basin below the pass.

## Sec. 2. Eastern Approach No. 7

### *South Fork of Bishop Creek*
### *(Inyo National Forest;*
### *Parcher's Camp-Bishop Pass Region)*

*Reached by auto:* Over California 168 from Bishop (Line St.) until reaching the forks, whence the south fork is taken to Habegger's Resort, Parcher's Camp, and South Lake, 22 miles from Bishop. Limited overnight parking at the roadhead; more two miles down the canyon.

*Accommodations:* Parcher's Camp Lodge; Habegger's Resort.

*Supplies:* Bishop, Habegger's, Parcher's.

*Saddle and pack stock, guides:* Rainbow Pack Train at Parcher's.

This east portal of the Sierra Crest has a beautiful alpine setting. The road climbs steadily out of Bishop to an altitude of nearly 10,000 feet at its terminus on South Lake, above which a chain of lakes continues almost to the crest. They occupy the huge amphitheater dominated on the east by the barren Inconsolable Range and on the west by Mts. Goode, Johnson, Gilbert, and Thompson, extending along the crest.

Bishop Creek is an ideal starting point for a circuit on the Muir Trail going in over Piute Pass and out over Bishop Pass, or vice versa. When stock is taken the return is close to the starting point, solving that problem, although a wide extent of mountain country has been covered on the trip. Taboose Pass is the next pass over the crest to the south.

## Sec. 3. Eastern Lateral No. 9

### *Bishop Pass Trail*

| *South Lake to Le Conte Canyon* | El. above Sea level | Dist. from pt. above | Total distance | |
|---|---|---|---|---|
| South Lake (Parcher's Camp) ...... | 9,750 | 0.0 | 0.0 | 13.0 |
| Bishop Pass...................... | 12,000 | 7.2 | 7.2 | 5.8 |
| Dusy Lakes...................... | 11,300 | 2.0 | 9.2 | 3.8 |
| Muir Trail (Le Conte Canyon) ...... | 8,700 | 3.8 | 13.0 | 0.0 |

The Bishop Pass Lateral is a very short and interesting approach to the Muir Trail from the east. About six hours on the trail took the energetic Starr from the end of the road, through some of the best scenic parts of the High Sierra, to the Muir Trail on the Middle Fork of the Kings River. Regular mortals coming from sea level might happily spend two days getting there.

The trail from Parcher's Camp follows south along the east side of South Lake and then climbs to the upper basin of lakes. Shut in by towering peaks and walls, it passes along the eastern shore of Long Lake and continues on past several smaller lakes. Inspiring views are enjoyed all along the route. From the upper end of the basin a short stiff climb brings you to the crest at

*Bishop Pass* (12,000—7.2). Just east of the pass rises the jagged Mt. Agassiz (13,882), easily climbed, with a wild view south along the Palisade peaks and down onto the north Palisade Glacier, largest in the Sierra.

In the basin below the pass lie

*Dusy Lakes* (11,300—2.0), where campsites and some grazing are to be found, along with an imposing view of the northern Palisade peaks. No wood fires are permitted in this basin above the first bridge on the trail.

From the Dusy Lakes the trail descends Dusy Creek. While descending we enjoy wonderful views looking across the upper canyon of the Middle Fork of Kings River, Le Conte Canyon. At the head of the canyon, which bends to the west, rises the Goddard Divide, which separates the headwaters of the Kings from those of the San Joaquin. Muir Pass is the only route across this divide. We come to the

*Muir Trail* (8,700—3.8) on the Middle Fork of Kings River.

## Sec. 4. Eastern Approach No. 8

*Big Pine Creek*
*(Inyo National Forest;*
*Big Pine Lakes-Palisade Glacier Region)*

*Reached by auto:* Over road (11 miles) from Highway 395 at Big Pine.

*Reached by bus:* Daily, to Big Pine between Los Angeles and Reno, and Big Pine to Glacier Lodge in season.

*Accommodations:* Big Pine, Big Pine Creek (Glacier Lodge).

*Supplies:* Big Pine, Big Pine Creek.

*Saddle and pack stock, guides:* Glacier Pack Train and Palisade School of Mountaineering, Big Pine Creek.

The region at the headwaters of the two forks of Big Pine Creek is another area that contains some of the grandest country to be found in the eastern approaches to the Sierra Crest. These two basins of lakes and glaciers, separated by a rugged ridge dominated by Temple Crag, are walled in by the towering knife-edged Palisade Crest, which here forms the backbone of the Sierra, rising to an elevation of over 14,000 feet. Along its summit are Mount Agassiz (13,891), Mt. Winchell (13,768), North Palisade (14,242), Mt. Sill (14,162), Middle Palisade (14,040). Under the northeast face of this crest lie a number of glaciers below Middle Palisade in the south fork basin. The Palisade Glacier occupies the upper end of the north fork basin under Mt. Sill, North Palisade, and Mt. Winchell. These are the most southerly glaciers in the United States, and the Palisade Glacier is the largest in the Sierra. A number of beautiful lakes lie in the basin of the North Fork.

Glacier Lodge and a public camp are in the canyon at the forks of Big Pine Creek near the end of the road. This is the starting point up either fork of Big Pine Creek. The North Fork road is now closed to overnight backpacker parking 1½ miles below the roadhead, where there is an auto camp. A trail leads up the North Fork 5 miles to the Big Pine Lakes and 10 miles to the Palisade Glacier. A faint old trail leads northeast to Coyote Flat from just below Black Lake. Experienced climbers can scale Mt. Winchell, Mount Agassiz, and Temple Crag, and seasoned rock-climbers, properly equipped, can climb the difficult and precipitous walls of Mt. Sill and North Palisade, but this is a blind canyon to walkers.

## Sec. 5. Western Approach No. 3B

### Crown Valley

Having come from the road which extends south of Wishon Dam and then the Crown Valley Trail to

Crown Valley (12.0) (enthusiastic visitors have, since the time of naming, reduced the crown to a balding dome, and a jeep road now threatens its imperial isolation as well). (See Part III, Secs. 12, 13.) We find here the junction of several trails. The old Tunemah Trail (41) takes off to the east leading to Blue Canyon and Tehipite Dome (see Sec. 7). From the east end of the meadow another trail branches north to Woodchuck Country, offering a fine loop of the North Fork of the Kings and coming back finally to Courtright Reservoir. Our trail goes south to enter the Kings Canyon National Park near Gnat Meadow and then drops down into the deep canyon of the Middle Fork of Kings River. Following up the river for 20 miles we meet the Muir Trail at the mouth of Palisade Creek.

### Sec. 6. Western Lateral No. 6

*Tehipite-Middle Fork Trail*

| *Crown Valley to Palisade Creek* | El. above Sea level | Dist. from pt. above | Total distance | |
|---|---|---|---|---|
| Crown Valley . . . . . . . . . . . . . . . . . . . . . | 7,900 | 0.0 | 0.0 | 29.5 |
| Gnat Meadow (Park Entrance) . . . . . | 7,450 | 5.0 | 5.0 | 24.5 |
| Tehipite Valley (Mid. Fork Kings R.) | 4,150 | 4.0 | 9.0 | 20.5 |
| Simpson Meadow (Trail Junction) . . . | 5,900 | 12.0 | 21.0 | 8.5 |
| Cartridge Creek Trail . . . . . . . . . . . . . | 6,400 | 4.2 | 25.2 | 4.3 |
| Muir Trail at Palisade Creek . . . . . . . . | 8,000 | 4.3 | 29.5 | 0.0 |

The Tehipite Trail is a long lateral passing through the middle Sierra region on its way to the high mountains. It offers opportunity to see the great canyon of the Middle Fork of Kings River, rivaling in grandeur and exceeding in depth the Kings Canyon of the South Fork. For a length of 12 miles the south wall of this great canyon rises over 6,000 feet from the river to the crest of the Monarch Divide, which separates the Middle and the South forks of the Kings. This mighty wall of rock is beautifully sculptured into spurs and gorges, presenting an inspiring panorama of Nature's architecture, over which the eye can roam while imagination constructs arches, spires, and cathedrals. The view is best from the north rim of Tehipite Valley, preferably from the top of Tehipite Dome or nearby (see Sec. 7).

Starting from Crown Valley (7,900—0.0) (see Sec. 5) our trail to Tehipite Valley goes south through a forested country. About a mile along our way, a trail branches southwest up Rodgers Creek to Spanish Mountain (10,051), a high point on Rodgers Ridge which separates the North Fork and the South Fork of Kings River. Here one looks down over 8,000 feet to the river from the highest canyon wall in America. Our trail continues southward to

*Gnat Meadow* (7,450—5.0) (known locally as Hay Meadow) on the north rim of the canyon, a good campsite before descending (overnight camping only). The next good campsite on the route is Simpson Meadow, the floor of Tehipite Valley being rather barren except early in the season. At Gnat Meadow it is worthwhile to walk about a mile out to a point a little north of east from the meadow, where one has a magnificent view from the canyon rim into the valley, with Tehipite Dome directly to the east, and the great south wall across the canyon.

From Gnat Meadow the trail soon starts down into the canyon over a rough zigzagging route and comes to the river at the lower end of

*Tehipite Valley* (4,150—4.0). The valley is a small widening of the canyon at the base of the dome, where Crown Creek comes down its canyon into the valley from the north over cascades and a waterfall known as Silver Spray Falls. Elsewhere the walls almost meet at the river and there the canyon has no floor such as that of Yosemite or Kings Canyon. It presents a clear, impressive example of stream erosion.

Tehipite Dome dominates the north wall of Tehipite Valley, rising a sheer 3,600 feet from the valley floor, with a majesty and beauty of shape and proportion all its own. Its only peer among Sierra domes is Half Dome in Yosemite. Tehipite is symmetrical and smoothly rounded.

Leaving the valley, the Middle Fork Trail follows the north bank of the river up its great canyon to

*Simpson Meadow* (5,900—12.0) where it crosses the river to its east bank and meets the Simpson Meadow Trail (43) which comes over the Monarch Divide from the South Fork of Kings River (see Sec. 8). From the trail junction we come up the river to a bridge over

*Cartridge Creek* (6,400—4.2) The old Cartridge Creek Trail which comes in just above here is abandoned and falling into disrepair. Not recommended. Above Cartridge Creek the canyon of the Middle Fork narrows until it becomes a deep, steep, rocky gorge through which the river descends in a tumult of whirling cataracts and wild cascades. At the mouth of Palisade Creek we meet the

*Muir Trail* (8,000—4.3) a mile below Grouse Meadows (see Sec. 1).

### Sec. 7. Tunemah Trail (41)

*Crown Valley to Blue Canyon
and Tehipite Dome*

This is an old sheep and cattle trail, and in the early days was used to reach Simpson Meadow via Tunemah Pass. (Total distance about 25 miles.) However, the trail beyond Alpine Creek has been seldom used for many years, and the route over Tunemah Pass down to Simpson Meadow is not recommended. Leaving Crown Valley at

*Collins Meadow* (7,900), the Tunemah Trail goes eastward, descending to and crossing

*Crown Creek* (7,000—3.5), where a lateral ascends the stream for some distance. Our trail climbs out over the ridge to the summit at the

*Base of Kettle Dome* (8,700—3.0). This is the point for hikers to leave the trail to climb Tehipite Dome. To do so follow south along the top of the ridge leading out to the dome, its summit being little higher than the ridge at its base. There is one short bad place to cross, where good boots and a rope will be very useful. You will find the view from the summit of the dome ample reward for the effort.

After climbing the dome, work your way northeast along the canyon rim for about a mile to a high point topped with large rocks. Here is a superb view of the tremendous south wall of the Middle Fork canyon. Unless required to return to the point of leaving the trail, you may contour around northward until you intersect the trail descending to Blue Canyon Creek.

From the top of the ridge below Kettle Dome our trail descends to

*Blue Canyon Creek* (7,500—2.0) and follows up the west bank of the stream. About half a mile upstream the old Tunemah Trail fords and climbs out of the canyon (trail overgrown and abandoned). The new route continues up the stream to

*Blue Canyon* (8,300—3.0), which is one of the most beautiful side canyons in this region. Good camping places are numerous. A trail goes on up the stream to its headwaters in a peak-encircled basin (10,000—2.5) containing half a dozen lovely lakes.

### Sec. 8. Simpson Meadow Trail (43)

| *Middle Fork to South Fork Kings R.* | El. above Sea Level | Dist. from pt. above | Total distance | |
|---|---|---|---|---|
| Simpson Meadow-Middle Fork Kings River | 5,900 | 0.0 | 0.0 | 28.0 |
| Horseshoe Lakes Trail | 9,900 | 7.0 | 7.0 | 21.0 |
| Dougherty Meadow | 9,500 | 1.0 | 8.0 | 20.0 |
| State Lakes Trail | 9,600 | 1.0 | 9.0 | 19.0 |
| Kennedy Canyon Trail | 9,500 | 1.0 | 10.0 | 18.0 |
| Granite Pass | 10,670 | 3.0 | 13.0 | 15.0 |
| Granite Basin | 10,000 | 1.0 | 14.0 | 14.0 |
| Kings Canyon at Copper Creek | 5,035 | 9.0 | 23.0 | 5.0 |
| Cedar Grove-South Fork Kings R. | 4,635 | 5.0 | 28.0 | 0.0 |

This is the best and most scenic way across the high divide between the Middle and South Forks of the Kings River.

Below the mouth of Goddard Creek where it enters the Middle Fork of Kings River, the canyon floor widens out into a valley and is known as Simpson Meadow. From *Simpson Meadow* (5,900—0.0) our trail strikes out, up along the steep ridge between

Horseshoe Creek and Dougherty Creek. At the crest of the ridge the

*Horseshoe Lakes Trail* (9,900—7.0) branches east to Horseshoe Lakes and State Lakes (see Lateral 43B below). A short descent brings us to

*Dougherty Meadow* (9,500—1.0) on the east fork of Dougherty Creek (good camping and grazing). Leaving the meadow the trail goes around and over a low divide, passing the junction of the

*State Lakes Trail* (9,600—1.0) branching east to State Lakes and Horseshoe Lakes (see Lateral 43B below), and at the Middle Fork of Dougherty Creek (camping and grazing) comes to the junction of the

*Kennedy Canyon Trail* (9,500—1.0) coming from the South Fork of Kings River (see Part V, Sec. 5). We follow up the stream and cross

*Granite Pass* (10,670—3.0) to

*Granite Basin* (10,000—1.0) (camping and grazing) from where we descend to the head of Copper Creek. At Tent Meadow (3.0) a trail (rough and difficult to follow) branches east to Paradise Valley on the South Fork of Kings via Goat Mountain (fine view). We follow down the west side of Copper Creek on the long zigzag descent to the floor of

*Kings River Canyon* (5,035—9.0) where we meet the trail coming up the canyon (WL 7, see Part V, Sec. 6) from

*Cedar Grove* (4,635—5.0).

*Lateral (43B)—Dougherty Meadow
to Horseshoe Lakes*

For its marvelous views, this is a never-to-beforgotten trip. There are two trails leading to Horse-shoe Lakes. One goes eastward from Dougherty Meadow to State Lakes (10,200—2.0) and thence northward to Horseshoe Lakes (10,500—2.0). The other leaves the Simpson Meadow Trail (43) at the summit of the ridge one mile north of Dougherty Meadow and goes east 2 miles to join the trail referred to above midway between State Lakes and Horseshoe Lakes. To the east is Windy Ridge, its northern end (B. M. 11,150) overlooking the great canyon of the Middle Fork of Kings River. From this vantage point a marvelous panorama is presented. The view sweeps across the canyon of Cartridge Creek beyond the basins and lakes at the headwaters of its tributary streams to the Palisades on the Sierra Crest. Northward the view is up the canyon of the Middle Fork to the peaks in the Muir Pass region, and to the rugged spurs and gorges of Goddard Creek. The view westward is directly down the grand canyon of the Middle Fork toward Tehipite.

# PART V:
# South Fork of
# Kings River Region

The Muir Trail here traverses an ideal route, keeping close to the crest. Many have enjoyed the inspiring beauty of this region of the High Sierra and much has been written describing the scenic gems to be found there. Lake Marjorie, Twin Lakes, and Rae Lakes, unexcelled in beauty, are passed on the way, and side trips may be taken to many other lakes and to peaks with outstanding views. Among them are Bench Lake, Pyramid Peak, Woods Lake, Dragon Lake, Sixty Lakes Basin, Mt. Clarence King, Charlotte Lake, Gardiner Creek Lakes, Kearsarge Lakes, University Peak, Center Basin. Formerly the great barrier of the Kings-Kern Divide made it necessary to drop down over Junction Pass to the east of the crest and then climb back again over Shepherd Pass to Bighorn Plateau. The trails and passes over the Kings-Kern Divide were too rough for pack stock. In 1932 a new trail was made over Foresters Pass which removes this difficulty.

## Sec. 1. The John Muir Trail

### *Mather Pass to Foresters Pass*

| Points on the Route | El. above Sea level | Dist. from pt. above | Dist. from Mather P. | Dist. to Frstr. P. |
|---|---|---|---|---|
| Mather Pass ..................... | 12,080 | 0.0 | 0.0 | 37.4 |
| Taboose Pass Trail Junction ........ | 10,000 | 5.4 | 5.4 | 32.0 |
| Bench Lake Trail Junction ......... | 11,000 | 1.1 | 6.5 | 30.9 |
| Lake Marjorie ................... | 11,200 | 1.5 | 8.0 | 29.4 |
| Pinchot Pass .................... | 12,100 | 1.5 | 9.5 | 27.9 |
| Twin Lakes ..................... | 10,560 | 3.1 | 12.6 | 24.8 |
| South Fork Trail ................. | 8,500 | 4.5 | 17.1 | 20.3 |

| Points on the Route | El. above Sea level | Dist. from pt. above | Dist. from Mather P. | Dist. to Frstr. P. |
|---|---|---|---|---|
| Rae Lakes (north end) . . . . . . . . . . . . . | 10,500 | 5.5 | 22.6 | 14.8 |
| Dragon Lake Trail . . . . . . . . . . . . . . . . | 10,550 | 1.0 | 23.6 | 13.8 |
| Sixty Lakes Basin Trail . . . . . . . . . . . . | 10,550 | 0.3 | 23.9 | 13.5 |
| Glen Pass . . . . . . . . . . . . . . . . . . . . . . . | 11,980 | 2.0 | 25.9 | 11.5 |
| Glen Pass Lake  . . . . . . . . . . . . . . . . . . | 11,500 | 0.8 | 26.7 | 10.7 |
| Junction Charlotte Lake-Gardiner Creek and Kearsarge Pass Trails . . | 10,800 | 1.5 | 28.2 | 9.2 |
| Bubbs Creek Trail (Vidette Meadow) | 9,600 | 2.2 | 30.4 | 7.0 |
| Center Basin Trail . . . . . . . . . . . . . . . . | 10,500 | 3.0 | 33.4 | 4.0 |
| Foresters Pass . . . . . . . . . . . . . . . . . . . | 13,200 | 4.0 | 37.4 | 0.0 |

From *Mather Pass* (12,080)

A long, zigzag descent brings us to the granite floor of Upper Basin, at the headwaters of the South Fork of Kings River. The floor of this upper basin contains a network of small tributary streams and lakes and some very interesting terminal and lateral moraines. We continue southward, parallel to the crest, down the western side of the basin, which gradually becomes more timbered. Later the eastern valley wall ends, a basin slopes upward to the crest at Taboose Pass, and the stream turns southwestward away from the crest. Here we come to a cut-off to the Taboose Pass Trail. We cross the infant Kings River to a junction of the

*Taboose Pass Trail* (5.4) (EL 11, see Sec. 3). We climb to the

*Bench Lake Trail* (11,000—1.1), which leaves our route to the west and goes southwestward along the valley rim to Bench Lake (10,640—2.5). Beyond this unique body of water (camping and grazing) rises the graceful pyramid of Arrow Peak, the most distinctive feature of the upper South Fork region, which may be climbed from the lake.

The Muir Trail proceeds up a long lake basin, passing several small lakes (fine grazing and scenic camping places) to

*Lake Marjorie* (11,200—1.5). Skirting above the eastern shore of this blue lake, our route continues past several high rock-bound lakes above it. Beyond the uppermost lake we ascend a steep rocky cliff, rather rough toward the top, to

*Pinchot Pass* (12,100—1.5), the summit of a spur ridge extending from the crest, separating the upper South Fork of Kings River and its tributary, Woods Creek. The view into the headwaters of Woods Creek is a grand one, particularly the high wall of dark forbidding peaks above Woods Lake.

From Pinchot Pass the trail descends a steep talus cliff to a high rocky basin at the headwaters of Woods Creek. Due to heavy use a one-day camping limit applies from here to Glen Pass. After passing several high open meadows and a small lake, we reach

*Twin Lakes* (10,560—3.1), lying below and southeast of the trail. Exceptional camping and grazing are found at these lakes, delightful in their impressive high mountain surroundings. A mile below the lakes we come to the junction of the old

*Sawmill Pass Trail,* which was always rough and is now no longer maintained.

Our route goes downstream on the northwest side of the canyon of Woods Creek, with its brilliantly tinted rocks and foaming cascades, to the junction of Woods Creek and its south fork. Just below is the junction of the

*South Fork (Kings River Canyon) Trail* (8,500—4.5). From here the well-constructed and much traveled trail via Paradise Valley (WL 7, see Sec. 6) goes down Woods Creek to Paradise Valley and Kings River Canyon. The Muir Trail fords Woods Creek and continues up the west bank of its south fork.

There are several good ready-made camp-spots near the junction of the trails and an excellent green meadow down the Paradise Valley Trail about a quarter of a mile below the ford and trail junction. The Muir Trail, after fording Woods Creek, follows up the west bank of its south fork along a large wooded valley. About 1.5 miles above Baxter Creek we pass a small round lake lying to the east of the trail.

From the lake our trail passes through meadows and along a chain of lakes. (The Rae Lakes Ranger Station is located above the trail at Middle Rae Lake. No wood fires are permitted from Lower Rae Lake to Glen Pass, and there is a one-day camping limit at all the lakes.) We continue on to the

*Northern end of Rae Lakes* (10,500—1.5). (No grazing of pack and saddle stock; allowed only north of the Baxter Creek Trail junction. Burros and walking mules allowed one night's grazing. No picketing of stock.) The trail skirts the eastern shoreline. Rae Lakes deserve the reputation of being the most beautiful high mountain lakes along the Sierra Crest. The graceful pinnacle of Fin Dome beyond the lower lake, the varicolored stripes upon the face of the crags above the upper lake, the beaches, promontories, bays, and islets, and the irregularity of the grassy shoreline, give the lakes unique charm. Shadow Lake from its lower end and Lake Ediza (see Part II, Sec. 1) rival Rae Lakes in beauty. The upper lakes are divided by a narrow promontory. Along this dividing strip of rock the trail crosses to the western shore via an improved crossing. The best campsites are on the eastern side of the lakes. The

*Dragon Lake Trail* (10,550—1.0) (ducked, rather rough and not easy to find) starts at the base of the cliffs east of the promontory mentioned. Dragon Lake lies about a mile east of the upper Rae Lake. (Grazing restrictions same as at Rae Lakes.) The peculiar dragon-shaped lines of the peak at its upper end give the lake its name. There is a notable view across the lower end of Dragon Lake toward Glen Pass.

From the west shore of Rae Lakes starts the

*Sixty Lakes Basin Trail* (10,550—0.3). From this point a ducked trail leaves our route and proceeds over the ridge south of Fin Dome into beautiful Sixty Lakes Basin (one-day camping and limited grazing), dominated by Mt. Clarence King and Mt. Cotter.

The Muir Trail skirts the western shoreline to the upper end of Rae Lakes and then climbs to the headwaters of a stream which feeds the lake in a rough rocky basin strewn with lakelets and surrounded by forbidding cliffs. Above is Glen Pass. The ascent to Glen Pass, on the Rae Lakes side, is difficult for stock when the snow has not been cleared and it should be scouted before taking animals across. The trail zigzags up a rocky ridge to the base of the cliffs over steep sliding rock, then up the cliff to the summit of the spur ridge which extends from the crest and divides the headwaters of Woods Creek from those of Bubbs Creek. Here is

*Glen Pass* (11,980—2.0), from the summit of which there is a fine view southward toward the rugged Kings-Kern Divide.

From Glen Pass we zigzag down a steep cliff by a fairly good trail, far less difficult than the Rae Lakes side, to a high rockbound lakelet which, because it has no official name, I shall call

*Glen Pass Lake* (11,500—0.8). We skirt the west shore and ford the stream (short-cut to Charlotte Lake ducked down this stream—passable for stock), then swing around a cliff to a level stretch. Here we come to the

*Junction of the Charlotte Lake-Gardiner Creek and Kearsarge Pass Trails* (10,800—1.5). To the west a short mile is Charlotte Lake (10,370). (One night camping, but no grazing allowed here or at the first big meadow below the lake. Grazing available down Charlotte Creek in the lower meadows.) From the lake a trail (47b) goes westward north of Charlotte Creek about 3 miles and then starts a mile climb northwestward over Gardiner Pass (11,200). (This trail is not maintained and should be avoided by stock parties.) From the pass it descends into the headwaters basin of the south fork of Gardiner Creek, and follows down a long chain of lakes on the east side (camping) to the north fork of the creek. The north fork is crossed and followed eastward up to its lakes in Gardiner Basin (total distance 11.0 miles). This trail explores a beautiful country of many lakes, with commanding peaks nearby to be climbed.

Leading east from the junction with the Charlotte Lake Trail, the Kearsarge Pass Trail (EL 14, see Sec. 3) crosses the bench above Bullfrog Lake and continues on to the junction of the trail leading down to Kearsarge Lakes. From here the trail goes due east to the crest at Kearsarge Pass, whence a descent of 4 miles brings you to Onion (Kearsarge) Valley, the end of the road from Independence.

We continue south on the trail which strikes off over

the rim of the canyon and descends steeply toward
Bubbs Creek. Near the end of a series of switchbacks,
a route heads northeastward, past a small lake, to
Bullfrog Lake, one of the most beautiful of Sierra waters. There is a memorable view from the upper end
across the lake to Mt. Brewer and to the graceful
pyramid of the West Vidette. Unfortunately, because
of overuse, Bullfrog Lake is now permanently closed
to camping.

At the junction of the trail to Bullfrog Lake, the
signs read: *(Muir Trail–north)* Kearsarge Pass 4 mi.,
Charlotte Lake 1½ mi.

We continue to zigzag down the wooded wall of the
valley of upper Bubbs Creek, enjoying charming vistas
through the trees of Center Basin, Mt. Brewer, and the
spires of the Videttes in the immediate foreground.
Upon reaching the valley floor we come to the junction
of the

*Bubbs Creek Trail* (9,600—2.2), which comes up the
canyon of Bubbs Creek (WL 8, see Sec. 7), at Vidette
Meadows.

The meadows along the stream for a considerable
distance above and below the junction of the trails
afford good camping and fair grazing grounds. A
beautiful side trip can be made from here up to Vidette
Lakes (3 miles), lying in the basin between East Vidette and West Vidette.

By following WL 8 down Bubbs Creek to Junction
Meadow (2.5 miles), one can take a trail (47) up East
Creek (see Sec. 7) to East Lake (starting point for Mt.
Brewer) and beautiful Lake Reflection. This trail leads
to one of the finest regions of them all. From here a
knapsack route crosses the Kings-Kern Divide over
Harrison Pass.

The Muir Trail ascends the northeast bank of Bubbs Creek to its headwaters under Junction Peak (13,888) on the Kings-Kern Divide, passing over beautiful meadows (camping and grazing) and through forests. After passing between the jagged Kearsarge Pinnacles on the east and the East Vidette on the west, grand views are offered of Deerhorn Mountain and Mt. Stanford, with their perpetual snowfields.

At the forks of Bubbs Creek below Center Peak is the junction of the

*Center Basin Trail* (10,500—3.0), which goes up the east fork to its string of fine lakes. Before Foresters Pass straightened it out, the Muir route went up this basin, over Junction Pass on the crest to descend a ways on the east side before crossing the crest again at Shepherd Pass to rejoin the present trail at Tyndall Creek. This roundabout route is no longer maintained.

Following the Muir Trail we ford the east fork of Bubbs Creek and continue south up the main stream, passing between Deerhorn Mountain and Center Peak. After crossing a tributary we ascend to an upper basin, pass a lake, and then climb the south rim of the basin to the top of the Kings-Kern Divide, just west of Junction Peak, at

*Foresters Pass* (13,200—4.0).


## Sec. 2. Eastern Approach No. 9

*Independence-Owens Valley*

*Reached by auto:* Over Highway 395.

*Reached by bus:* Daily between Los Angeles and Reno.

*Reached by airplane:* Terminals at Independence;

no scheduled flights.

*Accommodations:* Hotels and garages.

*Outfitting:* Supplies, guides, pack and saddle stock.

Two laterals lead to the Muir Trail from roads branching from Highway 395 near Independence:

(A) A road leaves the highway about 14 miles north of Independence and ends on the north side of Taboose Creek (6 miles). Here starts the Taboose Pass Trail (EL 11).

(B) A road leaves the highway at Independence and goes up Independence Creek via Grays Meadow to Onion (Kearsarge) Valley (pack station) (15 miles). Here starts the Kearsarge Pass Trail (EL 14).

## Sec. 3. Eastern Laterals Nos. 11 and 14

### *A–Eastern Lateral No. 11–Taboose Pass Trail* *Owens Valley to South Fork of Kings River*

Leaving the end of the road from Owens Valley (EA 9-A) (5,300—0.0), this trail winds up on the north side of Taboose Creek. This is a notably rocky route over talus slopes much of the way, but the old trail has been reconstructed. It is also a long dusty climb and no water is reached on the ascent until Taboose Creek is crossed at 8,500 feet. From here, however, it is a scenic route to Taboose Pass (11,360—7.0) (fine views of the canyon of the South Fork of Kings River in its rugged alpine setting) whence the trail descends through a basin to the John Muir Trail (10,000—3.0) near its junction with the Cartridge Creek Trail at the bend of the upper South Fork of Kings River. Total distance, 9.5 miles.

### B–Eastern Lateral No. 14–Kearsarge Pass Trail
### Onion Valley to Charlotte Lake-
### Gardiner Creek Trail Junction

From the road end at Onion Valley (EA 9-B)
(9,100—0.0) on Independence Creek, a good trail
climbs to its headwaters, passing four small lakes, and
crosses the crest at Kearsarge Pass (11,823—4.0).
From the pass the trail descends to the junction of the
trail leading down to Kearsarge Lakes (no wood fires;
one-day camping limit), then crosses the bench above
Bullfrog Lake (this badly overused lake has been permanently closed to camping for several years now to
study its ability to recover from heavy use), to meet
the Muir Trail at its junction with the Charlotte
Lake-Gardiner Creek Trail. This is the shortest, lowest, and easiest lateral over the crest in the Independence area.

### Sec. 4. Western Approach No. 4

#### Kings Canyon National Park

*Reached by auto:* From Fresno via Highway 180
and from Visalia via Highway 198 and the Generals
Highway or via Highway 69 to General Grant Grove.
Thence via the Kings River Highway to Cedar Grove
in Kings River Canyon.

*Reached by stage:* From Tulare and Visalia.

*Accommodations:* General Grant Grove and
Lodge; Meadow Camp (housekeeping tents and auto
camp); Cedar Grove, public campgrounds. Season
from May 25 to Sept. 5.

*Supplies:* Stores at Grant Grove and Cedar Grove.

*Saddle and pack stock, guides:* Cedar Grove, Grant Grove.

For information concerning Kings Canyon National Park ask park headquarters for copy of the Government pamphlet containing general information. This park contains two groves of big trees, saved from the lumberman out of the great groups of giant sequoias that once forested the basins on the south side of Kings River.

### Sec. 5. Kennedy Canyon Trail (43-C)

*From Kings River Canyon Over Monarch Divide to Simpson Meadow Trail*

This is a beautiful and little-used trail out of Kings Canyon.

From the ranger station at *Cedar Grove* (4,635—0.0) in Kings River Canyon, a trail ascends the great north wall by way of Wildman Meadow and Frypan Meadow on the long climb of over 6,000 feet to Kennedy Pass at the summit of the

*Monarch Divide* (10,800—9.0), the great mountain mass which separates the South Fork and Middle Fork of Kings River. While ascending the winding zigzags leading to the summit, inspiring views are presented into the great canyon and to the high mountain crests beyond. The pass is crossed just east of Kennedy Mountain (11,433). Marvelous views are enjoyed both north and south. The trail descends into the upper end of

*Kennedy Canyon* (10,000—1.0) with its lakes and meadows (camping and grazing). Proceeding northward down the canyon 3.5 miles, the trail then climbs the east wall formed by Dead Pine Ridge to the point of the ridge overlooking the great canyon of the Middle Fork of the Kings. From this ridge (high point 10,664) the panorama of canyons and peaks extending to the Sierra Crest is indescribably grand. The trail doubles back along the length of the ridge to its eastern side at

*Volcanic Lakes* (10,200—6.0), the headwaters of the West Fork of Dougherty Creek (camping and grazing). From the lakes the trail turns northward and then crosses a very low divide to the Middle Fork of Dougherty Creek where is met the

*Simpson Meadow Trail* (9,500—2.0) (see Part IV, Sec. 8) about 2 miles north of Granite Pass.

## Sec. 6. Western Lateral No. 7

### *South Fork (Paradise Valley) Trail*

| Cedar Grove to Woods Creek | El. above Sea level | Dist. from pt. above | Total distance | |
|---|---|---|---|---|
| Cedar Grove (Kings Canyon) . . . . . | 4,635 | 0.0 | 0.0 | 20.0 |
| Copper Creek | | | | |
| (Simpson Meadow Trail) . . . . . . . . | 5,035 | 5.0 | 5.0 | 15.0 |
| Bubbs Creek Trail . . . . . . . . . . . . . . . | 5,100 | 2.0 | 7.0 | 13.0 |
| Paradise Valley (Goat Mtn. Trail) . . . | 6,500 | 5.0 | 12.0 | 8.0 |
| Mouth of Woods Creek . . . . . . . . . . . | 6,900 | 3.0 | 15.0 | 5.0 |
| John Muir Trail, at Woods Creek . . . . | 8,500 | 5.0 | 20.0 | 0.0 |

There is a one-day camping limit the length of Paradise Valley, and no grazing. From

*Cedar Grove* (4,635—0.0) the South Fork Trail parallels the road in Kings River Canyon on the north side of the river. The south wall, rising 4,500 feet above the valley, presents many interesting features of rock sculpture, but lacks the awe-inspiring massiveness and depth of the canyon of the Middle Fork (Tehipite). Opposite Grand Sentinel, the most commanding cliff structure in the canyon, a trail (43) comes down Copper Creek from Granite Pass and Simpson

Meadow. This is the

*Simpson Meadow Trail* (5,035—5.0). (See Part IV, Sec. 8.)

The South Fork Trail continues on up the canyon to the junction of the

*Bubbs Creek Trail* (5,100—2.0) (WL 8, see Sec. 7). Here the Kings River bends at a right angle, and the trail proceeds north following the west bank, passing Mist Falls, to the lower end of Paradise Valley. Continuing up the west bank through Paradise Valley, our trail crosses the South Fork on a foot bridge one-half mile above the ford used by stock parties just above the

*Mouth of Woods Creek* (6,900—8.0), which enters from the east.

While there is no made trail from here up the South Fork, knapsackers frequently go up the narrow canyon between its great walls to the upper valley (8.0). Pack stock have been taken through, but only by experienced packers. The east wall of the canyon, known as Muro Blanco, which rises 4,000 feet to Arrow Ridge, presents a beautiful and remarkable picture of finely sculptured white granite. Our trail goes up Woods Creek on the north side of the canyon, and reaches the

*John Muir Trail* (8,500—5.0) at the forks of Woods Creek.

## Sec. 7. Western Lateral No. 8

### *Bubbs Creek Trail*

| *Cedar Grove to Vidette Meadows* | El. above Sea level | Dist. from pt. above | Total distance |
|---|---|---|---|
| Cedar Grove (Kings River Canyon) . | 4,635 | 0.0 | 0.0 |

| Cedar Grove to Vidette Meadows | El. above Sea level | Dist. from pt. above | Total distance |
|---|---|---|---|
| South Fork Trail Junction . . . . . . . . . | 5,100 | 7.0 | 7.0 |
| Sphinx Creek Trail . . . . . . . . . . . . . . . | 6,250 | 2.0 | 9.0 |
| East Lake Trail (Junction Meadow) . | 8,200 | 6.5 | 15.5 |
| John Muir Trail at Vidette Meadows . | 9,600 | 2.3 | 17.8 |

There is a one-day camping limit all the way up Bubbs Creek to Kearsarge Pass. Having arrived from Cedar Grove at the junction of the

*South Fork (Paradise Valley) Trail* (WL 7) (5,100—7.0), the Bubbs Creek Trail crosses Kings River on a bridge and proceeds up the north bank of Bubbs Creek. About 2 miles above the bridge the

*Sphinx Creek Trail* (6,250—2.0) comes down Sphinx Creek tributary (WL 9, see Sec. 10) to meet the Bubbs Creek Trail. (No grazing from here to Junction Meadow.) Continuing up the canyon on the north bank, we come to the

*East Lake Trail* (8,200—6.5) at Junction Meadow. This trail (47) starts up the west bank of East Creek and soon crosses to the east bank. Skirting around East Lake (9,445—3.0) (camping but no grazing) the trail continues up the east bank of the stream, passes a cascade, crosses the east fork and comes to a trail junction (10,200—1.2). The west-branching trail crosses the west fork and follows it to Lake Reflection (10,005—0.8), one of the most beautiful of lakes. The east-branching trail at the junction ascends a sandy cliff to a beautiful flat basin with lakelets and striking cliff surroundings. From here a rough trail ascends steeply upstream, fording three times, to the upper basin, passing between the lower two lakes and ascending to the highest lake at the headwaters. To the south a foot route climbs over talus to Harrison Pass

(12,700—4.0) (impassable to pack stock) leading to Lake South America and the Muir Trail at Tyndall Creek at the headwaters of Kern River (see Part VI, Sec. 7). An easier foot pass, Lucys Foot Pass (no trail), is just west of Mt. Ericsson.

From Junction Meadow we continue up Bubbs Creek to meet the

*John Muir Trail* (9,600—2.3) at Vidette Meadows.

### Sec. 8. Western Approach No. 5

*Horse Corral*
*(Sequoia National Forest)*

*Reached by auto:* From Fresno and Visalia via General Grant Grove (see Sec. 4), or via Giant Forest (see Part VI, Sec. 2). A road turns off from the Generals Highway about 8 miles south of General Grant Grove via Big Meadow.

*Reached by stage:* From Fresno.

*Accommodations:* Public campgrounds.

*Saddle and pack stock, guides.*

From the Generals Highway, a Forest Service road traverses Big Meadow (public campgrounds and Forest Service Guard Station), crosses the canyon of Boulder Creek to Horse Corral Pack Station (pack stock and guide service), and continues on to Horse Corral Meadow (7,650—10.6) and Government Corrals. Southward, a trail ascends to Marvin Pass (9,100), passing the junction of the Sheep Creek Trail from Summit Meadow. At the pass the trail branches east toward Sugarloaf Creek and south to Rowell Meadow. From the junction at Rowell Meadow, trails branch east to Scaffold Meadow (see Sec. 9), south-east to Silliman Pass (see Sec. 9), and south over J. O. Pass to Giant Forest (see Part VI, Sec. 3a).

A permanent timber access spur road goes east from the Government Horse Corral all the way to Summit Meadow (8,000—3.7), where a trail descends by switchbacks to the floor of Kings River Canyon at Cedar Grove. Near Summit Meadow is Lookout Peak (8,531), easily reached from the trail and affording a superb view of the Kings River Canyon.

## Sec. 9. Approach to Western Laterals 9, 10, 11

### *Horse Corral to Scaffold Meadow*

From Horse Corral this trail leads to a common starting point at Scaffold Meadow of three important laterals leading to widely separated destinations through beautiful high country: The Sphinx Creek Trail, Colby Pass Trail and Elizabeth Pass Trail. From

*Horse Corral* (7,650—0.0) the trail ascends to

*Rowell Meadow* (8,900—3.5), whence we travel east through meadowed, forested country (camping and grazing) and cross over Kanawyer Gap (9,600), an-other entrance to Kings Canyon National Park. Near

*Sugarloaf Creek* (8,000—2.0) we come to a junction with another trail coming from Horse Corral via Horse Corral Meadow and Marvin Pass (9,100), from where a lateral goes to Rowell Meadow. A south-branching trail goes up Sugarloaf Creek (camping and grazing) to Seville Lake (8,425—3.0). About a mile below the lake, we pass the junction of a trail from Rowell

Meadow and the trail that comes from a junction with the J. O. Pass Trail (see Part VI, Sec. 3a) via Silliman Pass (10,200) and Ranger Lakes (9,200). The latter trail provides another route to the Horse Corral-Scaffold Meadow Trail from the Lodgepole Ranger Station on the Generals Highway in Giant Forest. Proceeding eastward we follow Sugarloaf Creek branch of Roaring River to Sugarloaf Meadow, then continue 3.5 miles before crossing a low divide (a northerly ridge extending off Barton Peak) and continuing to the main stream at the

*Scaffold Meadow* (7,400—9.0) trail junction.

## Sec. 10. WL 9

### *Sphinx Creek Trail*

| *Scaffold Meadow to Bubbs Creek* | El. above Sea level | Dist. from pt. above | Total distance | |
|---|---|---|---|---|
| Scaffold Meadow ................ | 7,400 | 0.0 | 0.0 | 14.8 |
| Moraine Meadows ................ | 8,300 | 2.8 | 2.8 | 12.0 |
| Avalanche Pass .................. | 10,000 | 6.0 | 8.8 | 6.0 |
| Sphinx Creek .................... | 8,700 | 3.0 | 11.8 | 3.0 |
| Bubbs Creek Trail ............... | 6,250 | 3.0 | 14.8 | 0.0 |

The Sphinx Creek Trail from *Scaffold Meadow* (7,400—0.0) climbs the steep east canyon wall of Roaring River to *Moraine Meadows* (8,300—2.8) and then ascends northward over *Avalanche Pass* (10,000—6.0) between Palmer Mountain and Sphinx Crest. Thence a descent is made to *Sphinx Creek* (8,700—3.0). A branching trail goes up the west side of the stream to Sphinx Lakes (10,700—2.5), which lie in a deep glacier basin northwest of Mt. Brewer. After crossing the stream, our trail goes down the east side of Sphinx Creek (passing The Sphinx, a granite spire, at the end of a ridge to the west, from which stream and trail take the name), and then zigzags down the steep wall of the canyon, crosses Bubbs Creek, and meets the

*Bubbs Creek Trail* (6,250—3.0) (see Sec. 7).

## Sec. 11. WL 10

### *Colby Pass Trail*

| *Scaffold Meadow to Kern River* | El. above Sea level | Dist. from pt. above | Total distance | |
|---|---|---|---|---|
| Scaffold Meadow . . . . . . . . . . . . . . . . . | 7,400 | 0.0 | 0.0 | 22.0 |
| Colby Pass . . . . . . . . . . . . . . . . . . . . . | 12,000 | 13.0 | 13.0 | 9.0 |
| Kern-Kaweah River . . . . . . . . . . . . . . | 10,000 | 3.0 | 16.0 | 6.0 |
| Kern River (Junction Meadow) . . . . . | 8,000 | 6.0 | 22.0 | 0.0 |

From *Scaffold Meadow* (7,400—0.0) the trail ascends Cloud Canyon of Roaring River (stock limited to 12 head per party; grazing limited to 2 days), an easy ascent through forest and pleasing meadows, and follows the east fork up the east side to its headwaters in Colby Lake (campsites). This is one approach from which to climb Milestone Mountain. From the lake to Colby Pass the trail is quite rough and steep. The view of the Kaweah Peaks from the pass is one of the grand sights in the Sierra. From

*Colby Pass* (12,000—13.0) the southern descent is also quite steep and rough down to the basin below Milestone Bowl. This is another approach from which to climb Milestone Mountain. A stream is followed down the basin to its junction with the

*Kern-Kaweah* (10,000—3.0) below a small lake. The trail then descends the canyon, a very beautiful one (camping and grazing), to

*Junction Meadow (High Sierra Trail)* (8,000—6.0) (see Part VI, Sec. 4), through a scenic country, passing from meadow to meadow along the stream, spangled with colorful flowers in season, until it passes over a buttress by a steep defile, whence it goes down to the Kern.

## Sec. 12. WL 11

### Elizabeth Pass Trail

| Scaffold Meadow to Kaweah River | El. above Sea level | Dist. from pt. above | Total distance | |
|---|---|---|---|---|
| Scaffold Meadow . . . . . . . . . . . . . . . . | 7,400 | 0.0 | 0.0 | 17.0 |
| Elizabeth Pass . . . . . . . . . . . . . . . . . . . | 11,400 | 10.0 | 10.0 | 7.0 |
| Lone Pine Meadow . . . . . . . . . . . . . . | 9,000 | 4.0 | 14.0 | 3.0 |
| River Valley (High Sierra Trail) . . . . . | 7,600 | 3.0 | 17.0 | 0.0 |

From
*Scaffold Meadow* (7,400—0.0) we go up Roaring River on the west side and turn up Deadman Canyon fork, an easy gradual ascent through forest and meadow similar to Cloud Canyon. Big Bird Lake may be reached on foot by a short climb up its outlet stream. At the head of the upper, open, meadowed valley there is a very steep ascent to the left of some falls, with several rough places in the trail. It continues upstream, then cuts off to the right and up a stiff climb in talus to the top of the divide to

*Elizabeth Pass* (11,400—10.0). To get a good view, it is necessary to climb to a point above the pass. The descent is easy to

*Lone Pine Meadow* (9,000—4.0). A trail from the meadow runs east to Tamarack Lake and Lion Lake. Another trail ascends westward, then descends to Bearpaw Meadow and the High Sierra Trail.

The Elizabeth Pass Trail descends east of the stream to the

*High Sierra Trail* (7,600—3.0) (see Part VI, Sec. 4).

**Sec. 13. Simpson Meadow Trail (43)**

*From the South Fork
to the Middle Fork of Kings River*

Leaving the South Fork of Kings River in Kings Canyon at Copper Creek (5,035) about 5 miles up the canyon from Cedar Grove, this trail climbs over the Monarch Divide at Granite Pass (10,673) and descends to the Middle Fork of Kings River to meet the Tehipite-Middle Fork Trail at Simpson Meadow (5,900). Total distance from Copper Creek is about 23 miles. (For full description of the region traversed see Part IV, Sec. 8.)

# PART VI:
# Sequoia
# National Park Region

The Sequoia National Park region includes the headwaters of the Kern and Kaweah rivers, separated by the Great Western Divide, which extends north and south, parallel to the Sierra Crest, about midway across the park. Between the Sierra Crest and this great divide the Kern flows south. On the western slope of the divide the various forks of the Kaweah take their rise and flow westward, meeting just west of the park at Three Rivers to form the main stream. Scattered over the extensive basin of the Kaweah, in the western half of the park, are twenty-two groves of giant sequoias. The largest is called "The Giant Forest." John Muir wrote:

"I entered the sublime wilderness of the Kaweah Basin. This part of the Sequoia belt seemed to me the finest, and I then named it 'The Giant Forest.'"

What Yosemite is to the national park that bears its name, Giant Forest is to the Sequoia National Park. Both are reached by motor highways to the points where the High Sierra trails begin. Both were close to the heart of John Muir, who explored them and all the high region between.

Foresters Pass (13,200) is the highest pass on the Muir Trail excepting Trail Crest. The view north, extending to the Palisades and beyond, is one of the finest views from any pass in the Sierra. By ascending Junction Peak (13,888), a short distance to the east, a panorama even more remarkable is presented, for this peak occupies a strategic position at the junction of the Sierra Crest and the Kings-Kern Divide, offering an unobstructed sweep in all directions.

The view southward along the Sierra Crest includes the Whitney group of 14,000-foot peaks—the end of the grand crescendo of the Sierra. A short distance south the range loses rapidly in altitude and in grandeur. These 14,000-foot peaks are, from north to south: Williamson (14,375), just east of the crest; Tyndall (14,018), a graceful pyramid immediately west of

Williamson; Russell (14,086), immediately north of Whitney; Whitney (14,495), the highest peak in the United States excluding Alaska; Muir (14,015); and Langley (14,042).

The rugged peaks of the Kings-Kern Divide, extending westward from the crest at Junction Peak to Thunder Mountain, are a formidable barrier to high mountain travel between the Kings and the Kern. At Thunder Mountain the Kings-Kern Divide meets the Great Western Divide, a secondary crest extending southward parallel to the main Sierra Crest. The headwaters of the Kern River rise under the Kings-Kern Divide and flow southward between these two great crests—the Whitney group of 14,000-foot peaks on the east and the Great Western Divide on the west. On the Whitney side the main tributaries of the Kern, proceeding southward, are: Tyndall, Wallace, Whitney, Rock, and Golden Trout creeks. On the western side they are: Milestone Creek, the Kern-Kaweah, Big Arroyo, and Rattlesnake, Laurel, and Coyote creeks.

The Kaweah Peaks, one of the great groups in the Sierra, extend eastward from the Great Western Divide toward the Kern River, between the Kern-Kaweah and the Big Arroyo.

From Foresters Pass the Muir Trail traverses the high, sandy plateau between the eastern rim of the Kern Canyon and the Whitney group of peaks along the crest. The view of the Great Western Divide and the Kaweah Peaks from this plateau is a most impressive sight. At Wallace Creek the Muir Trail meets the High Sierra Trail from Giant Forest.

Stock parties are limited to 20 head in the park, and

loose herding is prohibited except where necessary for safety while crossing steep rocky sections of trail.

## Sec. 1. The John Muir Trail

### *Foresters Pass to Mt. Whitney*

| Points on the Route | El. above Sea level | Dist. from pt. above | Dist. from Frstr. Pass | Dist. to Whitney |
|---|---|---|---|---|
| Foresters Pass .................... | 13,200 | 0.0 | 0.0 | 24.8 |
| Tyndall Creek Trail ............... | 10,900 | 6.0 | 6.0 | 18.8 |
| High Sierra Trail ................. | 10,400 | 6.0 | 12.0 | 12.8 |
| Crabtree Ranger Station ........... | 10,700 | 4.5 | 16.5 | 8.3 |
| Mt. Whitney Trail ................ | 13,500 | 6.0 | 22.5 | 2.3 |
| Summit Mt. Whitney .............. | 14,495 | 2.3 | 24.8 | 0.0 |

### *Summit Mt. Whitney to Whitney Portal*

| | | | | |
|---|---|---|---|---|
| Trail Crest ........................ | 13,600 | 2.5 | | 2.5 |
| Whitney Portal (end of road) ........ | 8,360 | 8.2 | | 10.7 |

The Muir Trail descends from

*Foresters Peak* (13,200—0.0) on zigzags down a cliff to the high plateau of the Kern, and then goes southward down a basin, flanked on either side by a chain of lakes. By climbing to the top of a spur ridge which forms the western rim of the basin, a grand view may be had across the headwaters of the Kern to the Kaweah Peaks, to the Great Western Divide dominated by the slender spire of Milestone Mountain and the long flat top of Table Mountain, and to the Kings-Kern Divide. The Muir Trail descends the sloping plateau to

*Tyndall Creek Junction* (10,900—6.0). Here we meet the Tyndall Creek trail, which goes east to the old Shepherd Pass, and to the west descends Tyndall Creek to the Kern River (51), and the Lake South

America Trail (50) (see Sec. 7). Ascending from Tyndall Creek we pass a lake onto Bighorn Plateau. (Here, from a point about ½ mile southwest of and two hundred feet higher than a small lake near the trail, is one of the finest views in all directions to be found in the Sierra.) We cross Wright Creek and come to the forks of Wallace Creek where we meet the

*High Sierra Trail* (10,400—6.0) coming from Giant Forest (HST) (see Sec. 4). A trail (48) ascends Wallace Creek to Wallace Lake (11,470—5.0) and Wales Lake (11,732), both large lakes. This is the approach to climb Barnard and Russell.

We now travel across Sandy Meadow, a high sandy plateau with some grass and weather-beaten timber. We continue south to the junction on the ridge overlooking lower Crabtree Meadow. A cutoff trail continues downhill to the meadow, where it joins the trails from Army Pass (EL 18), Cottonwood-Siberian Pass (EL 19), and Golden Trout Creek (52), which come from the south as one trail, having met along the way. (See Secs. 11, 12, 13.)

The Muir Trail turns eastward at the junction, descending gradually to meet Whitney Creek just west of the

*Crabtree Ranger Station* (10,700—4.5). At the creek crossing we meet another trail coming up from Crabtree Meadow. Crabtree Meadow and the meadows above are popular base camps from which to start the ascent of Mt. Whitney. There are also feasible routes for knapsackers down Whitney Creek to the Kern River.

From the ranger station the trail goes east up Whitney Creek, passing several lakes under the southwest face of the mountain (Timberline Lake permanently closed to camping and grazing; trail closed to stock from one mile above Guitar Lake to Mount Whitney Summit), and climbs to the crest just south of Mt. Muir (the first peak south of Whitney), where we meet the

*Mt. Whitney Trail* (13,500—6.0), which comes from Whitney Portal on Lone Pine Creek. From the junction we work up a long steep talus slope to the summit of

*Mt. Whitney* (14,495—2.3), highest point in United States, excepting Alaska. We return on the Mt. Whitney Trail, passing the junction of the trail from the Crabtree Ranger Station, to the new pass at

*Trail Crest* (13,600—2.5) and descend the east side of the range to

*Whitney Portal* (8,360—8.2) at the end of the road from Lone Pine (see Secs. 9 and 10).

### Sec. 2. Giant Forest

*General Information*
*(Sequoia National Park;*
*Middle Fork of the Kaweah Region)*

*Reached by auto:* From Visalia via Highway 198 to Ash Mountain entrance, thence by the Generals Highway to Giant Forest. (Distance 52 miles.) From

Fresno by Highway 180 to General Grant Grove, thence by Generals Highway to Giant Forest. (Distance about 86 miles.)

*Reached by bus:* From Visalia and Tulare.

*Airplane:* From Visalia airport.

*Accommodations:* Giant Forest Lodge; housekeeping and auto camps; public campgrounds, all-year accommodations provided.

*Supplies:* Store.

*Saddle and pack stock, guides.*

Giant Forest, the largest of sequoia groves, is more a forest than a grove. Here stands the General Sherman Tree, said to be the largest living thing, measuring 36 feet at its greatest diameter and 272 feet high. There are many forest monarchs almost as large in the grove.

The Generals Highway connects Giant Forest with the General Grant Grove to the north. There it meets the Kings River Highway going to Kings River Canyon (see Part V, Sec. 4). The distance by the Generals Highway from grove to grove is about 30 miles.

## Sec. 3. Trails from Giant Forest

### (a) J. O. Pass and Silliman Pass Trails

From Lodgepole Ranger Station (6,720—0.0) on the highway 4 miles north of Giant Forest Village, a trail (44) ascends northward to cross the Silliman Crest at J. O. Pass (9,410—8.0) and descends to meet the Horse Corral-Scaffold Meadow Trail (see Part V, Sec. 9) at Rowell Meadow (8,800—3.0). About 2 miles south of J. O. Pass a lateral trail branches east and crosses Silliman Pass (10,200) to Ranger Lakes (9,200—3.0). From there a trail goes northward to Sugarloaf Creek which it descends to the Horse Corral-Scaffold Meadow Trail (8,000—6.0).

### (b) Pear Lake Trail

From the Wolverton parking area 3.5 miles north of

Giant Forest Village, a trail known as Lakes Trail ascends Wolverton Creek (7,000—0.0) to the junction with the Pear Lake Trail (7,900—2.0), which goes eastward along the rim of Tokopah Valley past Heather Lake and Emerald Lake and on to Pear Lake (9,510—5.0). No camping is permitted from the roadhead to Aster Lake. Above there, camp only in numbered campsites at Aster, Pear, and Moose Lakes. Stock is permitted for day use only.

### (c) Alta Peak–Moose Lake Trail

From the trail junction (7,900—2.0) on Wolverton Creek, this trail continues to the head of Wolverton Creek and then eastward along the upper wall of the great canyon of the Kaweah (passing the junction of a lateral going down to the High Sierra Trail—see Sec. 4), to Mehrten Meadow (9,000—3.5) (camping, closed to grazing). Here a trail branches north to the summit of Alta Peak (11,204—2.0), from which the view is a marvelous panorama of the Kaweah Basin and the Great Western Divide. Proceeding eastward our trail comes to Alta Meadow (9,000—2.0) (camping, closed to grazing) and then ascends to the ridge top, which is followed northward to Moose Lake (10,530—3.5) (camping, no grazing).

### Knapsack Route–Pear Lake to Moose Lake and Elizabeth Pass

From Pear Lake the route to Moose Lake is a loop via Table Meadows and then over a low divide to the headwaters of the stream flowing down Buck Canyon and fed by Moose Lake. There is also a short route directly across the divide separating the two lakes. From the divide it is possible to proceed eastward across the high plateau known as the Tableland and, after crossing a divide, to contour around the head of the canyon above River Valley to meet the Elizabeth Pass Trail (see Sec. 6 and Part V, Sec. 12), a short distance below the pass.

## Sec. 4. The High Sierra Trail (HST)

The High Sierra Trail is a well-graded trail from Crescent Meadow in Giant Forest to the head of Kern River, exploring a region rich in scenic grandeur. It crosses the Great Western Divide to the Kern River Canyon, which is then followed northward to above Junction Meadow, where the trail climbs the east wall of the canyon to meet the Muir Trail. Many important trails referred to in this section, from various approaches, join the High Sierra Trail along its route to meet the Muir Trail at Wallace Creek.

### *High Sierra Trail*

| *Giant Forest to Muir Trail at Wallace Creek* | El. above Sea level | Dist. from pt. above | Dist. from Cresc. M. | Dist. to Wal. Cr. |
|---|---|---|---|---|
| Crescent Meadow-Giant Forest .... | 6,700 | 0.0 | 0.0 | 49.1 |
| Junction Seven Mile Hill Trail ...... | 7,600 | 6.3 | 6.3 | 42.8 |
| Bearpaw Meadow (Junction of Timber Gap Trail) .............. | 7,800 | 4.7 | 11.0 | 38.1 |
| River Valley (Junction Elizabeth Pass Trail) ... | 7,600 | 2.0 | 13.0 | 36.1 |
| Hamilton Lake .................... | 8,235 | 3.0 | 16.0 | 33.1 |
| Kaweah Gap (Great Western Divide) | 10,700 | 3.7 | 19.7 | 29.4 |
| Big Arroyo (Trail Junction) ........ | 9,700 | 2.0 | 21.7 | 27.4 |
| Moraine Lake Trail-Chagoopa Plateau ............................. | 10,200 | 5.0 | 26.7 | 22.4 |
| Moraine Lake .................... | 9,290 | 2.6 | 29.3 | 19.8 |
| Sky Parlor Meadow .............. | 9,200 | 1.0 | 30.3 | 18.8 |

| *Giant Forest to Muir Trail at Wallace Creek* | El. Above Sea level | Dist. from pt. above | Dist. from Cresc. M. | Dist. to Wal. Cr. |
|---|---|---|---|---|
| High Sierra Trail Junction . . . . . . . . . . | 9,150 | 1.0 | 31.3 | 17.8 |
| Upper Funston Meadow (Kern R.) . . | 6,700 | 4.0 | 35.3 | 13.8 |
| Junction Meadow (Kern R.) . . . . . . . . | 8,000 | 9.0 | 44.3 | 4.8 |
| Muir Trail at Wallace Creek . . . . . . . . | 10,400 | 4.8 | 49.1 | 0.0 |

From Giant Forest Village a road leads 3 miles to

*Crescent Meadow* (6,700—0.0) (closed to grazing; no stock allowed on trail from here to Wolverton cutoff junction). Leaving the plateau of the Giant Forest the trail goes eastward high up on the great north wall of the canyon of Middle Fork of Kaweah River, over 3,000 feet above the stream. After proceeding about 6 miles we come to the junction of the

*Seven Mile Hill Trail* (7,600—6.3) which crosses our trail on its long climb from the Middle Fork-River Valley Trail (45) to the Alta Peak-Moose Lake Trail (see Sec. 3). We continue along the canyon wall and come to a side canyon, Buck Canyon. One-quarter mile west of Buck Canyon another trail branches north to climb up to the Moose Lake Trail (1.5). We cross Buck Canyon, climbing out on its eastern side to

*Bearpaw Meadow* (7,800—4.7) (ranger station and High Sierra Camp), where we come to the junction of the Timber Gap Trail (54) (see Alternate Route, page 182) coming up from the Kaweah River and Redwood Meadow and the trail to Elizabeth Pass and Lone Pine Meadow. (Nearest grazing is at Little Bearpaw Meadow.) Proceeding eastward, around the point of a ridge, we descend into Upper River Valley at the headwaters of the Kaweah. On the east bank is the junction of the

*Elizabeth Pass Trail* (7,600—2.0) (WL 11, see Sec. 6 and Part V, Sec. 12) which goes up the stream. From this point the region of our trail to Big Arroyo has unusual scenic attraction. We skirt around the point of a ridge to Hamilton Creek, cross the stream, and soon arrive at the lower end of beautiful

*Hamilton Lake* (8,235—3.0) (no grazing and no wood fires). Crossing the outlet, we climb the western slope of the Great Western Divide through the rugged, magnificent Hamilton Lakes region, passing north of the lakes, to the summit at

*Kaweah Gap* (10,700—3.7). From the pass our trail turns southward down to Big Arroyo, and a trail branches northward to Nine Lakes Basin whence there is a knapsack route over the Kaweah Peaks Ridge to the headwaters of the Kern-Kaweah, meeting the Colby Pass Trail, (WL 10, see Part V, Sec. 11). We descend along the stream between the Kaweah Peaks and Eagle Scout Peak and come to

*Big Arroyo Junction* (9,700—2.0) (approach to climb Black Kaweah). We meet the Big Arroyo Trail (55) (see Secs. 18, 19 and 20), coming up the canyon from Lost Canyon and Soda Creek, and the Black Rock Pass-Timber Gap Trail (53, 54), alternate route from Bearpaw Meadow and WL 12 (see Secs. 5, 16) from Mineral King via Little Five Lakes. Our trail leaves the stream, and gradually works up the northeast wall of the Big Arroyo to the Chagoopa Plateau. Near the head of Chagoopa Creek, on the plateau, we come to the junction of the

*Moraine Lake Trail* (10,200—5.0). Here a rough route leads northward up the Chagoopa Plateau, then crosses the Kaweah Peaks Ridge near a lake (12,328) just northeast of Mt. Kaweah (13,802), and descends through the Kaweah Basin to meet the Colby Pass

Trail (WL 10) on the Kern-Kaweah about 3 miles from Junction Meadow. This route discovers a glorious high region with remarkable views. (About 15 miles.)

The High Sierra Trail descends Chagoopa Creek, missing Moraine Lake, so we take the south-branching trail which makes a loop on an alternate route to

*Moraine Lake* (9,290—2.6), one of the gems of the mountains. From the lake it is but a short distance to

*Sky Parlor Meadow* (9,200—1.0), a vast expanse of greensward with borders framed by tall trees and red and silvery peaks (camping and grazing). (Water may be scarce late in the summer). From here a route (no longer maintained) descends the north wall of the Big Arroyo to the stream (7,700—1.5) and follows up the north bank about one mile to a junction with the Big Arroyo Trail (55).

From Sky Parlor Meadow we turn northward across the plateau to rejoin the

*High Sierra Trail* (9,150—1.0) near Chagoopa Creek and then turn back southward down the plateau (the views down Kern Canyon are very fine) to zigzag along Funston Creek into the Kern River Canyon north of

*Upper Funston Meadow* (6,700—4.0) (no grazing before June 15; thereafter 48 hour limit, no picketing in Kern Canyon) on the canyon floor, where we find grazing and good campsites. The Kern River Trail (49) goes down the canyon. It is 8.6 miles to Kern Canyon Ranger Station (campsites). Several laterals come up the Kern River Trail to meet the High Sierra Trail above Upper Funston Meadow: WL 15, WL 16, WL 17 (see Secs. 19, 20, 24).

Here we cross the Kern River and follow the trail

(the High Sierra Trail and Kern River Trail coincide to Junction Meadow) north along the east bank of the river. The floor of the valley above the meadow is level and gravelly without much grass. The Kern River Canyon holds to a remarkably true north and south course for a long distance. The canyon walls rise over 2,000 feet generally, but below the Red Spur of the Kaweah Peaks Ridge, the west wall rises 5,000 feet. We proceed up the canyon and come to the headwater forks of the Kern at

*Junction Meadow* (8,000—9.0) (closed to grazing). Wallace Creek comes in from the east and the Kern-Kaweah from the west. Down the latter comes the Colby Pass Trail (WL 10, see Part V, Sec. 11) having crossed Colby Pass on the Kings-Kern Divide from Cloud Canyon on Roaring River. The trail up Kern River continues on up the infant Kern River to Milestone Creek and Lake South America (see Sec. 7).

About one mile above the crossing of Wallace Creek in Junction Meadow the High Sierra Trail leaves the Kern River and climbs the east wall of the canyon working back toward Wallace Creek which it follows up to meet the

*Muir Trail* (10,400—4.8) near the crossing (see Sec. 1).

### *Alternate Route–Bearpaw Meadow to Big Arroyo via Timber Gap and Black Rock Pass Trails (54, 53)*

| *Bearpaw Meadow to Big Arroyo* | El. above Sea level | Dist. from pt. above | Dist. from Bpaw Mdw. | Dist. to B. Arroyo |
|---|---|---|---|---|
| Bearpaw Meadow (High Sierra Trail) | 7,800 | 0.0 | 0.0 | 19.3 |
| Middle Fork-River Valley Trail . . . . . | 6,000 | 2.7 | 2.7 | 16.6 |

| *Bearpaw Meadow to Big Arroyo* | El. above Sea level | Dist. from pt. above | Dist. from Bpaw Mdw. | Dist. to B. Arroyo |
|---|---|---|---|---|
| Redwood Meadow (Atwell-Redwood Trail) ......... | 6,000 | 1.6 | 4.3 | 15.0 |
| Black Rock Pass Trail Junction ..... | 7,000 | 3.5 | 7.8 | 11.5 |
| Pinto Lake ...................... | 8,700 | 3.0 | 10.8 | 8.5 |
| Black Rock Pass ................. | 11,600 | 3.5 | 14.3 | 5.0 |
| Little Five Lakes ................ | 10,500 | 2.0 | 16.3 | 3.0 |
| Big Arroyo (High Sierra Trail) ...... | 9,700 | 3.0 | 19.3 | 0.0 |

From *Bearpaw Meadow* (7,800—0.0), on the High Sierra Trail, a trail descends to the Kaweah River. After crossing this gently cascading stream the

*Middle Fork-River Valley Trail* (45) (6,000—2.7) is met coming up the Kaweah Canyon from the end of a road which leaves the highway at Hospital Rock Ranger Station (18.0). We follow downstream a short distance on this trail to the crossing of Eagle Scout Creek where our trail branches and ascends to a bench above the river at

*Redwood Meadow* (6,000—1.6) (limit 7 head of stock per party; grazing limit 48 hours), where we find a grove of giant sequoias and a ranger patrol cabin. Here a trail (68) branches westward from our route leading to the Atwell Grove of Big Trees, the Atwell Ranger Station (9.0) and Silver City, both on the road to Mineral King (see Sec. 15). Our trail (54) goes up the canyon of Cliff Creek to the junction of the

*Black Rock Pass Trail* (53) (7,000—3.5). The Timber Gap Trail (54) which we have been following, comes from Mineral King (see Sec. 16). We now proceed on the Black Rock Pass Trail up the canyon, which narrows and whose walls become cliffs. We ascend to a wide valley floor at its upper end and find a beautiful campsite with grazing nearby just above

*Pinto Lake* (8,700—3.0) at the head of an island

formed by the forking of the stream, having a fine view up the canyon and of the falls of Cliff Creek. After proceeding upstream more than a mile, our trail makes a switchback to the north side, and there starts the climb to the crest of the Great Western Divide. The ascent is long and rough, part way up zigzags on a talus cliff, but we are rewarded by the fine views of Upper Cliff Creek, Sawtooth Peak and Columbine Lake. We continue, crossing the summit at

*Black Rock Pass* (11,600—3.5). From the pass the view of Kaweah Peaks, Big Arroyo and Chagoopa Plateau is superb. We make a short steep descent to the barren upper lake of the group comprising Little Five Lakes. Passing west of a larger lake below, we come to an ideal campsite, with limited grazing nearby, at the head of a lower lakelet of

*Little Five Lakes* (10,500—2.0) from where there is a wonderful view across the lake to the Black Kaweah. From the eastern side of this lakelet a trail branches east to the basin of the Big Five Lakes. From here a knapsack route leads southwest to Columbine Lake and the Lost Canyon Trail (see Sec. 17). Proceeding on our trail northward we come to the Big Arroyo at

*Big Arroyo Junction* (9,700—3.0), where we meet the High Sierra Trail (see Sec. 4).

### Sec. 5. Middle Fork-River Valley Trail

*From Hospital Rock Ranger Station
to the Timber Gap Trail*

From Hospital Rock Ranger Station (2,800), on Highway 198 near the Middle Fork of Kaweah River, a road goes up the north side of the river 1.5 miles to Moro Rock Creek. Here starts the Middle Fork-River

Valley Trail (45) going up the canyon on its north side, the Seven Mile Hill Trail branching from it (see Secs. 3c and 4), until it crosses the Kaweah above its fork with Eagle Scout Creek (5,600) to meet the Timber Gap Trail (54) (see Sec. 4). Total distance from Moro Rock Creek about 17 miles.

## Sec. 6. Coppermine Pass Route

### Kaweah River to Kern River via Elizabeth, Coppermine and Colby Passes

Leaving the High Sierra Trail at River Valley on the headwaters of the Kaweah River (see Sec. 4), the Elizabeth Pass Trail (see Part 5, Sec. 12) may be taken to the pass. A knapsack route turns east along the crest of the Kings-Kaweah Divide and crosses a pass, known as Coppermine Pass, over Glacier Ridge (the divide between Deadman Canyon and Cloud Canyon) where it meets the Kings-Kaweah Divide. This rough trail descends into Cloud Canyon where it meets the Colby Pass Trail (see Part V, Sec. 11) which can then be taken over Colby Pass to the Kern-Kaweah and followed to the High Sierra Trail at Junction Meadow on the Kern River. Total distance about 28 miles.

## Sec. 7. Upper Kern Basin

### Lake South America-Harrison Pass

(a) From the junction with the High Sierra Trail one mile above
*Junction Meadow* (8,000) (see Sec. 4) the Lake South America Trail (50) continues up the infant Kern River, passing the
*Milestone Creek Junction* (10,600—5.0) about one-

half mile north of where the creek joins the Kern. The trail up Milestone Creek ascends the right (north) fork 2 miles to the lakes, lying under Milestone Mountain, at its source. This is a beautiful region.

Just above the Milestone Creek Junction is a notably fine campsite. Nearby a trail branches east to the Muir Trail (see b).

From the junction, the trail (rough) proceeds northward along a chain of lakes at the headwaters of Kern River to

*Lake South America* (11,941—4.0). Total distance about 8.5 miles.

(b) From

*Tyndall Creek* (10,950) (see Sec. 1), the trail to Lake South America (5) follows the Muir Trail north about a mile to a junction with a west-branching trail leading to the Kern River and Milestone Creek. We follow this trail west a short mile, passing south of a lake, to another trail junction. Here we head north, up the east side of a stream to the head of a long, grassy basin where a small lake reposes, above which we scale a short cliff to the summit of a divide. The view of the Kings-Kern Divide from here is sublime, extending from Mt. Stanford to Milestone Mountain. From the divide the trail descends to a small lake which feeds the head of the Kern and beyond we meet the northern end of the trail from Junction Meadow (see above) at a small lake south of

*Lake South America* (11,941—3.0).

(c) From *Lake South America* (11,941) the Harrison Pass route climbs a gentle, grassy slope at the head of the Kern Basin, passing between Mt. Ericsson on the west and Mt. Stanford to the east (a tall, dark cliff with two pointed pinnacles at the crest) through

*Harrison Pass* (12,700—2.0). This is the approach to ascend Mt. Stanford. The view from the pass is exceptionally good—northward to the Palisade Crest, southward to Milestone Mountain and the Kaweah Peaks. The difficulty and danger of Harrison Pass depends to a great extent on snow conditions. It should not be attempted without thorough scouting and is never suitable for large parties of any kind. The south approach is easy. The north side has two approaches—one by ledges next to the Ericsson cliff, the other toward Stanford, down a slippery rock slide or chute. Below is half a mile of rough large talus down a basin to the lower small lake. Seen from a descent of the pass, the views of Brewer and South Guard are very fine. Harrison Pass is impassable for pack stock. (Lucys Foot Pass, west of Mt. Ericsson, is an easier route.)

In the basin below the pass is found the end of the East Lake Trail (47) (see Part V, Sec. 7), leading to Lake Reflection, East Lake and Bubbs Creek.

### Sec. 8. Eastern Approach No. 10

*Lone Pine*

*Reached by auto:* Highway 395.

*Reached by bus:* Daily between Los Angeles and Reno.

*Reached by airplane:* Airport at Lone Pine; no scheduled flights.

*Accommodations:* Good motels at Lone Pine.

*Supplies:* Lone Pine, Whitney Portal Store.

*Pack and saddle stock, guides:* Lone Pine.

A road leaves the highway at Lone Pine and extends up Lone Pine Creek to Whitney Portal, starting point of the Mt. Whitney Trail (Muir Trail route) to the summit of Mt. Whitney. Distance to end of the road, about 12 miles.

### Sec. 9. Mt. Whitney Trail

From the end of the road on Lone Pine Creek (Whitney Portal—8,360) the Mt. Whitney Trail ascends over a well-graded winding trail to the summit of Mt. Whitney via Trail Crest (new pass). The total distance is about 10.7 miles, with a climb of over 6,000 feet. This trail is much traveled and a spectacular one, crossing the highest pass over the crest (13,600). The new pass is north of the old Whitney Pass (13,335), and, owing to its altitude, in seasons of heavy snowfall it may not be open for stock early in the summer.

The Mt. Whitney Trail is the route of the John Muir Trail from the summit of Mt. Whitney to its end at Whitney Portal.

### Sec. 10. Eastern Approach No. 11

#### *Cottonwood Creek*

Several good roads lead to Cottonwood Creek. One goes south from Lone Pine Creek two miles west of Lone Pine. Another leaves Highway 395 four miles south of Lone Pine; seven miles farther south on Highway 395 a road goes west four miles to a trail which follows up Cottonwood Creek to meet the upper road end southwest of Wonoga Peak. From here trails go over New Army Pass and Cottonwood Pass to cross the crest and meet again on Rock Creek, a tributary of Kern River, whence a trail goes north to meet the Muir Trail near Crabtree Meadow.

## Sec. 11. Eastern Lateral No. 18

### *Army Pass Trail*

(a) Where Little Cottonwood Creek (9,360—0.0) crosses the road from Lone Pine (on the slope of Wonoga Peak), a trail ascends Little Cottonwood Creek to its head and then descends to the main stream near Golden Trout Camp. Cottonwood Creek is followed to its headwaters at Cottonwood Lakes (11,000), whence a short but steep climb is made to New Army Pass (12,300—10.0).

(b) At the end of the road from Lone Pine on Cottonwood Creek (9,500), a trail follows up Cottonwood Creek all the way to its headwaters at Cottonwood Lakes and on to New Army Pass.

(c) From the lower road end on Cottonwood Creek (5,300—0.0), reached by driving south of Lone Pine on Highway 395 (see Sec. 10), a trail follows up Cottonwood Creek to the upper road end (9,500), and then along the same trail to

*New Army Pass* (12,300—14.0). From the pass the trail descends westward for 2 miles to a junction with a trail coming due north from Siberian Pass. It turns north for 2 miles, then descends Rock Creek to a junction with the Siberian Pass Trail (9,700—7.0). The united trails turn northward to the junction of the Muir Trail at the Crabtree Ranger Station (10,700—7.5).

## Sec. 12. Eastern Lateral No. 19

### *Cottonwood Pass-Siberian Pass Trail*

About one quarter mile above the upper road end (9,500—0.0) on Cottonwood Creek (see Sec. 11b), at the junction of the Army Pass Trail, which forks to the right, we come to the Cottonwood Pass Trail. Following the trail to the left, we cross a sloping plateau and then make a short steep climb to Cottonwood Pass (11,200—4.0). From the pass the trail descends one of the headwater forks of Golden Trout Creek to a trail junction in Big Whitney Meadow (9,800—3.5), where the trail from Kern River and Kern Lake, via Golden Trout Creek (52), comes in from the south. From the meadow the trail turns north, crossing a divide at Siberian Pass (10,900—3.0). Here a trail branches north to meet the Army Pass Trail in upper Rock Creek. Our trail descends westward down Siberian Pass Creek to meet the Army Pass Trail (9,700—5.0) lower down in Rock Creek. From this junction the united trails turn northward through Guyot Flat and on to the junction with the Muir Trail at the Crabtree Ranger Station (10,700—7.5). The total distance from the upper Cottonwood Creek road end is about 23 miles.

### Sec. 13. Golden Trout Creek Trail (52)

*Kern River to the Muir Trail
at Crabtree Ranger Station*

Just north of the Kern Canyon Ranger Station (6,458) a trail crosses the river, climbs the eastern wall and follows Golden Trout Creek (passing the junction of a trail to Rocky Basin Lakes (10,800—6.0) at Little Whitney Meadow) to its headwaters at Big Whitney Meadow (9,800—16.0), where we meet the Cottonwood Pass-Siberian Pass Trail (EL 19, see Sec. 12), which is then followed north to a junction with the Muir Trail at the Crabtree Ranger Station (10,700—15.5), the total distance being about 32 miles.

## Sec. 14. Western Approach No. 6

*Mineral King*
*(Sequoia National Forest;*
*East Fork of the Kaweah Region)*

*Reached by auto or stage:* From Visalia over Mineral King Road (mountain road), leaving Highway 198 at Hammond and ending at Mineral King in the Sequoia National Game Refuge just west of the Great Western Divide. Distance from Hammond, about 25 miles.

*Accommodations:* Summer resort, public camp, auto camp.

*Supplies, saddle and pack stock, guides.*

*Mineral King* (7,830) has beautiful high mountain surroundings. There are five different routes which may be taken through country with real scenic attraction leading to the Muir Trail: The Timber Gap-Black Rock Trail, WL 12; Lost Canyon Trail, WL 13; Soda Creek Trail, WL 14; Rattlesnake Creek Trail, WL 15; Farewell Gap-Coyote Pass Trail, WL 16. Interesting circuits can be worked out over this system of trails and connecting laterals.

## Sec. 15. Atwell-Redwood Trail (68)

From the Mineral King road at Atwell Ranger Station (6,500), this trail winds through the Atwell Grove of Big Trees while ascending northward to the divide (8,500) between the East Fork and the Middle Fork of the Kaweah River. From the divide the trail descends to Cliff Creek where is met the Timber Gap Trail (54) at Redwood Meadow (6,000—9.0) (see Sec. 5).

### Sec. 16. Western Lateral No. 12

*Timber Gap-Black Rock Pass Trails*
*Mineral King to Big Arroyo*

From *Mineral King* (7,830—0.0) the Timber Gap Trail (54) climbs over the divide separating the Middle and East forks of the Kaweah River, at
*Timber Gap* (9,400—2.5) and descends into Cliff Creek Canyon to meet the
*Black Rock Pass Trail* (53) (7,000—3.5) (see Sec. 5) which is then followed eastward to the High Sierra Trail at
*Big Arroyo Junction* (9,700—11.5). Total distance, 17.5 miles.

### Sec. 17. Western Lateral No. 13

*Lost Canyon Trail-Mineral King to Big Arroyo*

This trail finds beautiful country. From Mineral King the Sawtooth Trail goes eastward, ascending a tributary flowing out of Monarch Lakes, and, just below them, turns northward on its climb over a divide to the lakes at the head of Cliff Creek. From Monarch Lakes the ascent of Sawtooth Peak (12,343) is made. The divide is crossed at
*Sawtooth Pass* (11,700—4.0) (fine view) over a cirque, usually filled with snow in early summer, to beautiful
*Columbine Lake* (10,900—1.0). Snow conditions sometimes render the trail impassable until late July. Just east of the lake the trail crosses a pass on the Great Western Divide (11,000), descends Lost Canyon and, near its mouth, crosses over to join the Soda

Creek Trail (see Sec. 18) on which it descends a short
distance to meet the
*Big Arroyo Trail* (55) (8,000—6.0) at the stream.
That trail may be followed upstream to the
*Big Arroyo Trail Junction* (9,700—9.5) where is met
the High Sierra Trail (HST) (see Sec. 4). Total distance about 20 miles.

*or*

trail 55 may be followed downstream for a short distance and thence up the south canyon wall and over a
plateau to meet the
*Rattlesnake Creek Trail* (8,200—3.5) (see Sec. 19).
Total distance about 15 miles.

*or*

knapsackers may continue downstream from where
trail 55 leaves the canyon, for about a mile, and then
climb the north wall of the canyon to
*Sky Parlor Meadow* (9,200—2.5) (see Sec. 4). Total
distance about 14 miles.

## Sec. 18. Western Lateral No. 14

### *Soda Creek Trail*
*Mineral King to Big Arroyo*

From *Mineral King* (7,830—0.0) the trail goes
south, following up the east bank of the East Fork of
the Kaweah River and crossing Franklin Creek, which
flows out of Franklin Lakes. About a mile beyond this
crossing, we meet the
*Farewell Gap Trail* (8,800—2.3) (60) (see Sec. 20)

which continues south toward Farewell Gap. The Soda Creek Trail forks to the east, ascending a ridge south of Franklin Creek and later crossing back to the east side below

*Franklin Lakes* (10,200—2.3) from where it climbs over the Great Western Divide from the basin of the lower lake at

*Franklin Pass* (11,700—1.5). We descend to the head of Rattlesnake Creek, where the trail branches at the junction of the

*Rattlesnake Creek Trail* (10,300—1.0). From the junction an old trail goes south, over Shotgun Pass, to the Coyote Pass Trail (WL 16, see Sec. 20). The Rattlesnake Creek Trail (WL 15, see Sec. 19) continues east down the creek and the Soda Creek Trail strikes northeastward to the head of Soda Creek at

*Little Claire Lake* (10,400—1.6). The trail descends the canyon of Soda Creek and is joined by the Lost Canyon Trail (see Sec. 17) near the mouth of the canyon before arriving at

*Big Arroyo* (8,000—5.4). Here we meet the Big Arroyo Trail (55). The total distance to this point is about 13 miles. (For the choice of routes from here see Sec. 17.)

### Sec. 19. Western Lateral No. 15

*Rattlesnake Creek Trail*
*Mineral King to Kern River*

From *Mineral King* (7,830—0.0) this lateral follows the same route as WL 14 (see Sec. 18) to the

*Junction of the Soda Creek and Rattlesnake Creek Trails* (10,300—6.1). From there it descends Rattlesnake Creek and comes to the junction of the

*Big Arroyo Trail* (8,200—8.6) which branches north across a plateau and descends into Big Arroyo (8,000—3.5) less than a mile below the mouth of Lost Canyon. This trail (55) continues all the way up Big Arroyo from which it takes its name.

From the junction on Rattlesnake Creek, our trail zigzags down the steep canyon wall of the Kern to the

*Kern River Trail* (6,580—2.0) (49) which is followed to

*Upper Funston Meadow* (6,700—2.5), just south of the junction of the High Sierra Trail (see Sec. 4). This route is much used, although scenically inferior to the routes farther north. Total distance about 20 miles.

## Sec. 20. Western Lateral No. 16

### Farewell Gap-Coyote Pass Trails
### Mineral King to Kern River

From *Mineral King* (7,830—0.0) the Farewell Gap Trail (60) goes south up the East Fork of Kaweah River. The trail continues up the river from the junction of the Franklin Pass-Soda Creek Trail (WL 14) and climbs over the divide at

*Farewell Gap* (10,587—4.0) to the headwaters of the Little Kern River which it descends to the

*Little Kern River Trail Junction* (8,900—3.0). The Little Kern River Trail (56) continues down the stream and many laterals come into it. Trails 61 and 62 come from Clough Cave (WA 7) (see Sec. 21). Trails 58 and 59 come north to join 61 and 62, having come from Wishon Camp and Shake Camp (WA 8) (see Sec. 23).

From the junction the Coyote Pass Trail (WL 16) leaves the river, branching eastward along the slope of the Great Western Divide, crossing several small tributaries on the way. One of these tributaries is

*Shotgun Creek* (8,725—2.0) where an old trail, a lateral to Rattlesnake Creek, crosses the divide at Shotgun Pass (11,400), and descends to Rattlesnake Creek (10,300—5.0) at the junction of the Rattlesnake Creek Trail (WL 15, see Sec. 19) and the Soda Creek Trail (WL 14, see Sec. 18).

The Great Western Divide is crossed at

*Coyote Pass* (10,000—6.0), from which Coyote Creek is followed down to the Kern Canyon. The trail zigzags down the canyon wall and meets the Kern River Trail (49) above Kern Lake at the

*Kern Canyon Ranger Station* (6,456—6.0). The Kern River Trail is then followed up the canyon past Lower Funston Meadow (good camping and grazing) to

*Upper Funston Meadow* (6,700—8.6), just south of the junction of the High Sierra Trail. Total distance about 32 miles.

## Sec. 21. Western Approach No. 7

*Three Rivers and Clough Cave*
*(Sequoia National Park;*
*South Fork of the Kaweah Region)*

This approach to the headwaters of the Kern was much used before new routes made the upper Kern River region more accessible from other points.
*Three Rivers:*

*Reached by auto:* From Visalia over Highway 198 (distance 26 miles).

*Accommodations:* Motels, trailer park, camping; restaurant; post office.

*Supplies:* Store.

*Saddle and pack stock, guides:* Three Rivers, by special arrangement.

From Three Rivers a road ascends the South Fork of the Kaweah 12 miles to Clough Cave Ranger Station. From here a trail (63) works up the southern slope above the river through the Garfield Grove of Big Trees to the Hockett Lakes and the extensive meadows which cover the wide plateau. Here is the junction of the other trails: The Atwell-Hockett Trail (64) and the Eden Grove Trail (65) from the Mineral King road, and the Shake Camp-Hockett Trail (59) from the end of a road at Shake Camp (see Sec. 23). Another trail, the Cahoon Trail, goes to Hockett Meadows (15.0) by a route north of the river from Clough Cave.

From Hockett Meadows the route to the Kern is by way of Quinn Patrol Cabin or by Wet Meadows to Little Kern River. Trails come in from Wishon Camp and from Shake Camp, having made a junction with the Dennison-Sheep Mountain Trail (61), an alternate route from Garfield Grove to Quinn Patrol Cabin. At the Little Kern River Junction the Farewell Gap Trail (60) comes downstream from Mineral King (see Secs. 14-20), and the Little Kern Trail (56) comes upstream from WL 17 (see Sec. 24). The route from this junction to the Kern is via the Coyote Pass Trail (WL 16, see Sec. 20).

## Sec. 22. South Fork-Hockett-Little Kern Trails (63-62)

*Clough Cave to Little Kern River Junction*

At the end of the road from Three Rivers on the South Fork of the Kaweah River is

*Clough Cave Ranger Station* (3,500—0.0), just inside Sequoia National Park. From here starts the South Fork Trail (63) winding up the south side of the canyon through the Garfield Grove of Big Trees to the

*Hockett Lakes* (8,500—10.5) on the wide plateau at the headwaters. Beyond is a trail junction at

*Sand Meadows* (8,500—1.0), where is met the trail from Hockett Meadows. From Sand Meadows our trail (62) turns southward to

*South Fork Meadows* (8,500—1.0) (48 hour grazing limit with more than 12 head of stock). Two miles beyond at Green Meadow the trail branches, with the north fork going to the Little Kern River by way of Wet Meadows. From it a trail branches north to Blossom Lakes (3.5). The south-branching trail proceeds via Windy Gap, where it is joined by trails from WA 8 (see Sec. 23), to

*Quinn Patrol Cabin* (8,350—4.0), a historic cabin no longer manned by the Park Service. From here we turn northward to the Little Kern River, then follow upstream to

*Little Kern River Junction* (8,900—4.0) where is met WL 16 (see Sec. 20). Total distance about 23 miles.

### Sec. 23. Western Approach No. 8

*Shake Camp–Wishon Camp–Quaking Aspen*
*(Sequoia National Forest;*
*Headwaters of Tule River Region)*

*Shake Camp:*
*Reached by auto:* By road from Exeter via Milo (distance, 45 miles) or by Highway 190 from Porter-

ville via Springville and road via Milo (distance, 45 miles).

*Accommodations:* Auto camp, public camp.

*Supplies, saddle and pack stock.*

*Wishon Camp:*

*Reached by auto:* By Highway 190 from Porterville via Springville (distance, 30 miles).

*Accommodations:* Resort with cabins, auto camp, public camp.

*Supplies.*

*Quaking Aspen:*

*Reached by auto:* By road from Porterville via Springville and Camp Nelson (distance, 43 miles).

*Accommodations:* Lodge, auto camp, public camp.

*Supplies, saddle and pack stock.*

From these approaches several trails take off, connecting with various routes to the headwaters of the Kaweah and the Kern. All these approaches are also connected by trails.

From *Shake Camp* the Shake Camp-Hockett Trail (59) goes north to Hockett Lakes (10.0). Midway a trail branches east, to meet trail 61, going to Quinn Patrol Cabin on the way to Little Kern River (16.0). From here various routes may be taken (see Sec. 20).

From *Wishon Camp* the little-used Wishon-Little Kern Trail (58) climbs out of the canyon over the Tule-Little Kern Divide. Arriving at the summit, the trail forks, the north branch going via Quinn Patrol Cabin to Little Kern River Junction (20.0) (see Sec. 20), and the south branch to the Nelson-Kern Lake Trail (WL 17) at Burnt Corral Meadows (13.0).

From *Quaking Aspen* the Kern Lake Trail (WL 17, see Sec. 24) goes eastward to the Kern.

## Sec. 24. Western Lateral 17

*Kern Lake Trail–Quaking Aspen to Kern River*

From *Quaking Aspen* (7,000—0.0) the Kern Lake Trail goes northward along the Tule-Kern Divide for about 4 miles to a trail forks. The north branch follows down Clicks Creek to

*Burnt Corral Meadows* (6,000—10.0) on Little Kern River, and the south branch follows Fish Creek, crosses the Little Kern, and meets our route again near Trout Meadows. From Burnt Corral Meadows the trail proceeds eastward, along a plateau north of Little Kern to

*Trout Meadows* (6,121—7.0) (public pasture) on a tributary of that stream. Trout Meadows are followed northward up the peculiar long, straight, narrow valley (which skirts the extreme southern end of the Great Western Divide) to its head. Here the trail descends to

*Kern River* (5,789—6.5), which is followed up the west side to

*Kern Lake* (6,231—4.0), formed in the bed of Kern River by a natural dam deposited by a huge landslide. Going up the floor of the canyon the Coyote Pass Trail (WL 16, see Sec. 20) is met at

*Kern Canyon Ranger Station* (6,456—2.5). The Kern River Trail (49) is followed 3 miles up the canyon to Lower Funston Meadow (good camping and grazing) and continues on to

*Upper Funston Meadow* (6,700—8.6), just south of where we meet the High Sierra Trail (see Sec. 4). Total distance, about 39 miles.

## Sec. 25. Western Approach No. 9

### Kernville and Durrwood
### (Lower Kern River Region)

*Reached by auto:* Highway 178 to Kernville from Bakersfield and Mojave. Road up Kern River from Kernville to Durrwood, about 4 miles above Fairview. Distance: Bakersfield to Kernville, 53 miles; Mojave to Kernville, 75 miles; Kernville to Durrwood, 25 miles. This road now extends to Lloyd Meadow.

*Accommodations:* Hotel, auto camps, public camps.

*Supplies, pack and saddle stock, guides.*

From Durrwood a trail ascends Kern River to Lloyd Meadow (big trees). Most of the way it goes along the plateau above the river and to the west of it. From the meadows a trail leads northward to join the Kern Lake Trail (WL 17, see Sec. 24) near Trout Meadows, which is followed to the Kern River, where we take the Kern River Trail to Upper Funston Meadow. The distance from Durrwood to the High Sierra Trail above Upper Funston Meadow is about 43 miles.

# Sierra Trails

The trail routes into and across the Sierra Nevada found by early American pioneers were those which had long been used by Indians. The mountains had not been explored or entered by the Californians living near the coast during the earlier period of Spanish and Mexican occupation. These Indian trails evidently afforded means of crossing the mountains for the purpose of trading between tribes living east and west of the range, and perhaps for the less peaceful purpose of raids by the more warlike Indians of the eastern side.

To cross the northern part of the High Sierra region, the Mono Trail ascended the western slope of the mountains from Mariposa via Wawona and Alder Creek to the meadows of Bridalveil Creek, where the trail forked. A branch descended to Yosemite Valley via Inspiration Point. The Mono Trail descended to Mono Meadow, crossed Illilouette Creek and ascended to Starr King Meadow, where it turned back at the rim of Little Yosemite to descend to the Merced River, which it crossed about one mile above Nevada Fall. From there to Tuolumne Meadows the trail followed the present route of the Sunrise and Soda Springs Trail (the John Muir Trail route from Yosemite to Tuolumne Meadows). The old Indian trail then ascended Dana Fork of the Tuolumne River to cross over (northern) Mono Pass south of Mount Gibbs and descended Bloody Canyon to Mono Lake, in the land of the Mono Tribe of Indians.

Owens Valley was the home of the Piute Indians. They used (southern) Mono Pass, Piute Pass and

Kearsarge Pass to cross the range on the routes of the present trails.

While the early mining prospectors used and improved these trails, and built a few others, it was the sheep and cattle men who were responsible for much of the trail system of the Sierra Nevada, especially on its western slope. Excepting parts of the John Muir Trail, the High Sierra Trail, and some laterals which have been improved or relocated, most of the Sierra trails just happened—in moving livestock to and from summer ranges in high mountain meadows.

In Yosemite National Park, especially in the Tuolumne River watershed, United States Cavalry troops cleared and improved many of the cattle trails by use, and located some new trails, while on patrol duty in protecting Yosemite before the National Park Service came into being.

Soon after organization of the Sierra Club in 1892, Theodore S. Solomons conceived the idea of a trail along the backbone of the High Sierra, keeping as near to the crest as possible. As already noted, the existing trails crossed the range. Rugged canyons and passes rendered a trail along the range difficult. From 1892 to 1897 Solomons with other members of the Sierra Club made extended trips of exploration, principally in the upper branches of the San Joaquin River and the Merced.

In 1898 Joseph N. LeConte took up the quest for a High Sierra trail route. For many years thereafter, assisted by a few other members of the Sierra Club, he explored the canyons and the passes of the Kings and the Kern, and climbed many of the peaks along the crest.

In 1914 a committee of its members was appointed by the Sierra Club to enlist the help and cooperation of the State of California in the construction of a High Sierra Trail along the range. This committee was composed of Meyer Lissner (chairman), Walter L. Huber, David P. Barrows, Vernon L. Kellogg, and Clair S. Tappaan. Soon thereafter the President of the Sierra Club, John Muir, died, and it was decided to name the proposed trail "The John Muir Trail" as a fitting memorial. As a result of the efforts of the committee the California state legislature appropriated $10,000 to finance work on the trail in 1915.

The responsibility of selecting the route and spending the funds was given to the State Engineer, Wilbur F. McClure. Basing his decision on the information obtained by the many explorations of the past twenty years, principally by members of the Sierra Club, as well as on observations of his own made in the field, McClure selected the route now followed by the completed trail as the official route of the John Muir Trail from Yosemite Valley to Mount Whitney. To solve the problems of trail construction he wisely secured the cooperation of the Forest Service and arranged to have actual trail construction done under the management and supervision of its officers. This the men of the Forest Service accomplished through the years, faithfully and efficiently, with the meager funds at their disposal for such a large undertaking. Additional appropriations of $10,000 were made by the legislature in each of the years 1917, 1925, 1927, and 1929 as the result of Sierra Club efforts. Here ended the era of state assistance in the building of the John Muir Trail.

To complete the trail on its official route there now

remained two sections to be constructed over difficult passes. One of them, from the Kings to the Kern over Foresters Pass, was completed in 1932 by the National Park Service on the Kern River side of the divide and by the Forest Service on the Kings River side. The last section, up Palisade Creek at the headwaters of Middle Fork of Kings River and over Mather Pass to the headwaters of the South Fork of Kings River, was completed in 1938 by the Forest Service as the result of an appeal made to Regional Forester S. B. Show by the High Sierra Trails committee of the Sierra Club, through its chairman. Forest Supervisors Booth, Benedict, and Elliott, of the Inyo, Sierra, and Sequoia national forests, cooperated to accomplish this work. Shortly thereafter the region containing this section of the trail was transferred to the jurisdiction of the National Park Service by the creation of Kings Canyon National Park. Thus the John Muir Trail finally came to be, some forty years after it was conceived.

Another important trail to render the high mountain regions of the Kern and the Kaweah accessible was built in 1930-1931 by the National Park Service in Sequoia National Park under the supervision of Superintendent John R. White. Known as the High Sierra Trail, it starts at Crescent Meadow in Giant Forest, crosses the Kern-Kaweah divide to Kern River and meets the John Muir Trail on Wallace Creek tributary.

The trails of the High Sierra are now the responsibility of the National Park Service and the Forest Service. The work to be done each year on maintenance is most important. Both services have always lacked sufficient funds, earmarked in their budgets for trail maintenance, to do the job of keeping the trails decently passable. Individuals who travel on the trails can help in this effort by noting where trails are washed out, blocked by fallen trees, or otherwise badly in need of repair, while out on their summer trips, and reporting the information to the Forest Service and the National Park Service for their attention.

Naturally, the standards of trails in the Sierra trail system differ greatly and consideration must be given to their origin as described. On some of the main routes of travel, especially where trails have been made or relocated by the Park Service or Forest Service, standards are generally fairly good, but on many laterals and secondary trails such standards should not be expected. Parties traveling over the trails can help to maintain them by staying on the trail and not making short cuts, especially on switchbacks. Few realize the harm done by this practice. Maintenance can also be greatly helped by removing obstacles, if possible, instead of going around them with animals.

One of the original purposes of the club was to render mountain regions accessible. The club feels that this purpose has now been accomplished; that no more roads should be constructed in the wilderness area of the High Sierra extending from Yosemite National Park to Walker Pass; and that, with very few possible exceptions, no more trails should be constructed. To future generations of mountaineers should be left the pleasure, thrill, and experience of pioneering and finding their own routes to the many high mountain basins, lakes, and peaks which abound in this great wilderness.

WALTER STARR

# Index

# The John Muir Trail

## Yosemite Valley to Mt. Whitney

| Points on the Route and Trail Junctions | El. above Sea level | Dist. from pt. above | Total distance | | Page |
|---|---|---|---|---|---|
| *Yosemite National Park Region* | | | | | |
| Happy Isles ....................... | 4,035 | 0.0 | 0.0 | 211.9 | 36 |
| Mist Trail ....................... | 4,550 | 1.0 | 1.0 | 210.9 | 36 |
| Nevada Fall—Panorama Trail ..... | 5,950 | 2.3 | 3.3 | 208.6 | 36 |
| Little Yosemite— Merced Lake Trail .............. | 6,150 | 1.4 | 4.7 | 207.2 | 36 |
| Half Dome Trail ................... | 7,000 | 1.5 | 6.2 | 205.7 | 36 |
| Clouds Rest Trail ................. | 7,200 | 0.5 | 6.7 | 205.2 | 37 |
| Merced Lake High Trail .......... | 8,100 | 1.9 | 8.6 | 203.3 | 37 |
| Forsyth Trail to Tenaya Lake ...... | 8,150 | 0.1 | 8.7 | 203.2 | 37 |
| Long Meadow—Sunrise Camp ..... | 9,400 | 5.0 | 13.7 | 198.2 | 37 |
| Echo Creek Trail ................. | 9,450 | 1.0 | 14.7 | 197.2 | 37 |
| Cathedral Pass ................... | 9,700 | 1.0 | 15.7 | 196.2 | 38 |
| Cathedral Lake Trail .............. | 9,500 | 2.1 | 17.8 | 194.1 | 38 |
| Tuolumne Meadows— trail junction ................... | 8,550 | 3.0 | 20.8 | 191.1 | 38 |
| Glen Aulin Trail—Soda Springs .... | 8,600 | 1.5 | 22.3 | 189.6 | 39 |
| Tuolumne Meadows Ranger Station ....................... | 8,700 | 1.6 | 23.9 | 188.0 | 39 |
| Dana Fork—Parker Pass Trail ..... | 8,700 | 0.8 | 24.7 | 187.2 | 69 |
| Tuolumne Pass Trail .............. | 8,750 | 0.9 | 25.6 | 186.3 | 69 |
| Vogelsang Pass Trail ............. | 8,800 | 4.2 | 29.8 | 182.1 | 70 |
| Lyell Base Camp ................. | 9,000 | 3.0 | 32.8 | 179.1 | 70 |
| Donohue Pass ................... | 11,050 | 3.9 | 36.7 | 175.2 | 71 |
| *Rush Creek Region* | | | | | |
| Rush Creek Trail to Silver Lake ..... | 9,600 | 3.1 | 39.8 | 172.1 | 88 |
| Island Pass ...................... | 10,250 | 1.2 | 41.0 | 170.9 | 77 |
| *Middle Fork San Joaquin River Region* | | | | | |
| Thousand Island Lake ............. | 9,850 | 2.0 | 43.0 | 168.9 | 78 |

| Points on the Route and Trail Junctions | El. above Sea level | Dist. from pt. above | Total distance | | Page |
|---|---|---|---|---|---|
| Garnet Lake ...................... | 9,700 | 1.7 | 44.7 | 167.2 | 79 |
| Shadow Creek Trail ............... | 9,200 | 2.9 | 47.6 | 164.3 | 93 |
| Shadow Lake (upper end) .......... | 8,750 | 1.1 | 48.7 | 163.2 | 94 |
| Rosalie Lake ..................... | 9,500 | 1.5 | 50.2 | 161.7 | 81 |
| Gladys Lake ..................... | 9,600 | 0.7 | 50.9 | 161.0 | 81 |
| Johnston Lake—<br>Minaret Creek Trail ............. | 8,150 | 3.5 | 54.4 | 157.5 | 81 |
| Mammoth Trail ................... | 7,550 | 1.8 | 56.2 | 155.7 | 82 |
| Middle Fork San Joaquin River ..... | 7,500 | 0.2 | 56.4 | 155.5 | 82 |
| Devils Postpile ................... | 7,550 | 0.2 | 56.6 | 155.3 | 82 |
| Reds Meadow .................... | 7,600 | 0.7 | 57.3 | 154.6 | 82 |
| Mammoth Pass Trail .............. | 8,700 | 1.4 | 58.7 | 153.2 | 83 |
| Lateral to Mammoth Pass Trail ..... | 8,900 | 1.3 | 60.0 | 151.9 | 95 |
| Red Cones Trail .................. | 8,700 | 0.2 | 60.2 | 151.7 | 83 |
| Lateral to Mammoth Pass Trail ..... | 8,900 | 0.9 | 61.1 | 150.8 | 83 |
| Deer Creek (Mammoth Crest) ...... | 9,200 | 2.0 | 63.1 | 148.8 | 83 |
| Duck Lake Trail .................. | 10,100 | 5.2 | 68.3 | 143.6 | 83 |
| Purple Lake—trail to Fish Creek ... | 9,900 | 2.4 | 70.7 | 141.2 | 83 |
| Lake Virginia .................... | 10,300 | 1.7 | 72.4 | 139.5 | 84 |
| Tully Hole—McGee Pass Trail ..... | 9,500 | 2.0 | 74.4 | 137.5 | 84 |
| Cascade Valley Fish Creek Trail .... | 9,100 | 1.2 | 75.6 | 136.3 | 84 |
| Goodale Pass Trail ............... | 10,300 | 2.7 | 78.3 | 133.6 | 84 |
| Silver Pass...................... | 10,900 | 1.6 | 79.9 | 132.0 | 85 |
| *South Fork San Joaquin*<br>*River Region* | | | | | |
| Silver Pass Lake ................. | 10,350 | 0.6 | 80.5 | 131.4 | 103 |
| North Fork Mono Creek ........... | 8,900 | 3.0 | 83.5 | 128.4 | 103 |
| Mono Pass Trail .................. | 8,300 | 1.4 | 84.9 | 127.0 | 103 |
| Mono Creek Bridge ............... | 7,700 | 1.6 | 86.5 | 125.4 | 104 |
| Bear Ridge ...................... | 9,950 | 4.6 | 91.1 | 120.8 | 104 |
| Bear Creek Trail .................. | 8,800 | 2.1 | 93.2 | 118.7 | 104 |
| Lake Italy Trail .................. | 9,250 | 2.3 | 95.5 | 116.4 | 105 |
| East Fork Lakes Trail ............. | 9,500 | 1.2 | 96.7 | 115.2 | 105 |
| Marie Lake ...................... | 10,600 | 2.6 | 99.3 | 112.6 | 106 |
| Selden Pass ..................... | 10,870 | 1.3 | 100.6 | 111.3 | 106 |
| Heart Lake ...................... | 10,490 | 0.7 | 101.3 | 110.6 | 106 |
| Sally Keyes Lake ................. | 10,200 | 0.8 | 102.1 | 109.8 | 106 |
| Short-cut to Blayney Meadows ..... | 10,100 | 0.5 | 102.6 | 109.3 | 106 |

| Points on the Route and Trail Junctions | El. above Sea level | Dist. from pt. above | Total distance | | Page |
|---|---|---|---|---|---|
| Senger Creek | 9,700 | 1.7 | 104.3 | 107.6 | 107 |
| Blayney Meadows Trail | 7,800 | 3.8 | 108.1 | 103.8 | 107 |
| Piute Pass Trail | 8,050 | 1.7 | 109.8 | 102.1 | 107 |
| Aspen Meadow | 8,300 | 1.5 | 111.3 | 100.6 | 107 |
| South Fork Bridge | 8,350 | 1.3 | 112.6 | 99.3 | 107 |
| Goddard Canyon Bridge—Junction Hell-for-Sure-Pass Trail | 8,450 | 0.8 | 113.4 | 98.5 | 108 |
| Evolution Meadow | 9,200 | 2.0 | 115.4 | 96.5 | 108 |
| McClure Meadow | 9,600 | 2.0 | 117.4 | 94.5 | 108 |
| Colby Meadow | 9,800 | 1.0 | 118.4 | 93.5 | 109 |
| Evolution Lake—lower end | 10,850 | 3.5 | 121.9 | 90.0 | 109 |
| Evolution Lake—upper end | 10,850 | 1.3 | 123.2 | 88.7 | 110 |
| Muir Pass | 11,955 | 4.5 | 127.7 | 84.2 | 110 |
| *Middle Fork Kings River Region* | | | | | |
| Helen Lake | 11,595 | 1.0 | 128.7 | 83.2 | 131 |
| Le Conte Canyon—Upper Lake Camp | 10,800 | 1.3 | 130.0 | 81.9 | 131 |
| Little Pete Meadow | 8,800 | 4.5 | 134.5 | 77.4 | 132 |
| Bishop Pass Trail | 8,700 | 0.5 | 135.0 | 76.9 | 132 |
| Grouse Meadows | 8,200 | 3.2 | 138.2 | 73.7 | 133 |
| Palisade Creek—Middle Fork Trail | 8,000 | 1.0 | 139.2 | 72.7 | 133 |
| Deer Meadow—lower end | 8,700 | 3.5 | 142.7 | 69.2 | 133 |
| Palisade Lake | 10,650 | 3.0 | 145.7 | 66.2 | 134 |
| Mather Pass | 12,080 | 4.0 | 149.7 | 62.2 | 135 |
| *South Fork Kings River Region* | | | | | |
| Taboose Pass Trail | 10,000 | 0.2 | 155.1 | 56.8 | 149 |
| Bench Lake Trail | 11,000 | 1.1 | 156.2 | 55.7 | 149 |
| Lake Marjorie | 11,200 | 1.5 | 157.7 | 54.2 | 150 |
| Pinchot Pass | 12,100 | 1.5 | 159.2 | 52.7 | 150 |
| Twin Lakes | 10,560 | 3.1 | 162.3 | 49.6 | 150 |
| South Fork Trail | 8,500 | 4.5 | 166.8 | 45.1 | 150 |
| Rae Lakes—north end | 10,500 | 5.5 | 172.3 | 39.6 | 151 |
| Dragon Lake Trail | 10,550 | 1.0 | 173.3 | 38.6 | 152 |
| Sixty Lakes Basin Trail | 10,550 | 0.3 | 173.6 | 38.3 | 152 |
| Glen Pass | 11,980 | 2.0 | 175.6 | 36.3 | 152 |
| Glen Pass Lake | 11,500 | 0.8 | 176.4 | 35.5 | 153 |

| Points on the Route and Trail Junctions | El. above Sea level | Dist. from pt. above | Total distance | | Page |
|---|---|---|---|---|---|
| Junction Charlotte Lake and | | | | | |
| Kearsarge Pass Trails ........... | 10,800 | 1.5 | 177.9 | 34.0 | 153 |
| Bubbs Creek Trail ................ | 9,600 | 2.2 | 180.1 | 31.8 | 154 |
| Foresters Pass ................... | 13,200 | 7.0 | 187.1 | 24.8 | 155 |
| *Sequoia National Park Region* | | | | | |
| High Sierra Trail— | | | | | |
| Wallace Creek ................. | 10,400 | 12.0 | 199.1 | 12.8 | 174 |
| Crabtree Ranger Station ........... | 10,700 | 4.5 | 203.6 | 8.3 | 174 |
| Army Pass Trail ................ | — | — | — | — | 189 |
| Cottonwood Pass Trail .......... | — | — | — | — | 189 |
| Siberian Pass Trail .............. | — | — | — | — | 189 |
| Golden Trout Creek Trail ........ | — | — | — | — | 190 |
| Mt. Whitney Trail ................ | 13,500 | 6.0 | 209.6 | 2.3 | 175 |
| Summit Mt. Whitney .............. | 14,495 | 2.3 | 211.9 | 0.0 | 175 |
| *Summit Mt. Whitney to Whitney Portal* | | | | | |
| Trail Crest Pass .................. | 13,600 | 2.5 | — | 2.5 | 175 |
| Whitney Portal—Lone Pine Road ... | 8,360 | 8.2 | — | 10.7 | 175 |